OBSOLESCENCE AND PROFESSIONAL CAREER DEVELOPMENT

OBSOLESCENCE AND PROFESSIONAL CAREER DEVELOPMENT

H. G. Kaufman

amacom

A Division of American Management Associations

International standard book number: 0-8144-5344-9
Library of Congress catalog card number: 73-85187

FIRST PRINTING

FOREWORD

THIS IS a useful book that I commend to business managers on several counts. It deals with an important subject, the obsolescence of professionals, that looms large in a company's assets and liabilities even though accountants are unable to write in the appropriate numbers for it in the balance sheet. Secondly, the role of professionals in modern enterprises is growing both absolutely and relatively, which underscores that the subject will be even more important tomorrow than it is today.

As the author makes crystal clear, management is not without resources to affect the outcome—to determine whether the talents and capacities of its professional staff are to lose a smaller or larger part of their value through obsolescence. There is nothing inevitable in either the short or long run about the effectiveness of professional personnel. It all depends on how well the organization attends to the following:

- Monitoring obsolescence.
- Improving selection and assignment.
- Engaging in career assessment.
- Establishing flexible retirement policies.
- Making professional jobs more challenging.
- Using job assignments to avoid narrow specialization.
- Permitting career change for obsolescent professionals.
- Encouraging colleague interactions through work group structuring.
- Selecting competent supervisors.
- Creating an organizational climate that encourages personal growth.

· Planning and evaluating continuing educational programs.

These guidelines provide a clue to the broad approach that
Professor Kaufman has used to explore his subject, and they
also attest to his judiciousness and realism. Unlike so many
who offer advice to managers, he has avoided the trap of
arguing on the one hand that his subject is complex while
at the same time coming forward with a simple, gadgety solution. He insists that the problem of professional obsolescence
be studied in its natural habitat—that is, in live organizations
which through their policies and procedures determine how
professionals are selected and assigned; how their work is
structured and rewarded; how their careers are shaped by top
management and by their supervisors. If widespread obsolescence among professionals is a major characteristic of contemporary organizations to which high individual and enter-
prise costs attach, then remedial action can succeed only to the
extent that the causes of the obsolescence are correctly assessed,
only to the extent that responsive remedies are introduced.
And it is to Professor Kaufman's credit that he does not
minimize the difficulties of diagnosis or the complexities of
corrective action.

Having made clear my positive evaluation of this work, I
have two further comments. The writer has a felicitous style.
Unlike so many books on management, this one is substantially
free of jargon—that poor substitute for straight thinking.
Moreover, the book has a useful bibliography so that those
who want to probe these complex matters further can do so
without having to spend undue time in the library.

As a long-time student of human resources, I also see this
book from another perspective. Professor Kaufman believes
that obsolescence among professionals is a serious problem. I
agree. He stresses that professional education and training are
costly to both the individual and society, and rapid obsolescence therefore implies high individual and social costs. I
agree. He stresses that the way in which organizations deal

with their professional manpower determines whether obsolescence is accelerated or retarded. I agree. Finally, he insists that there are a large number of sound organizational policies and programs which, if introduced and pursued, can contain obsolescence. I agree.

What it all comes down to is this:

The key to an organization's efficiency is the way in which it conserves and uses its talent. The neglect of professional obsolescence is a risk that no management can willingly assume. It must be guarded against with vigor.

ELI GINZBERG

PREFACE

THIS BOOK is about the obsolescence of people. If we allow ourselves to think about it, we are all obsolescent in one way or another. The focus of this book, however, is the obsolescence of knowledge and skills among people who are professionals. Although my discussion of causes and cures of obsolescence may be relevant to diverse professional groups, I am not especially concerned here with those who are self-employed, such as doctors and lawyers, or with academically based teachers. These are important groups that deserve study in themselves. Rather, I am concerned with the millions of managerial, technical, and professional employees whose specialized knowledge and skills provide the direction and support which can make the difference between success and failure in business, industrial, and governmental organizations.

This book is directed primarily at the practicing manager. It should also be of interest to professionals employed in organizations and to the educators and counselors who provide the knowledge and guidance necessary for the launching and development of professional careers. In fact, its approach and content also make it appropriate for courses in a variety of fields ranging from personnel management to career guidance and development. The book's unusual versatility was attained by integrating the most up-to-date empirical knowledge available from research relevant to obsolescence with the practical experiences of managers and professionals. I felt this dual approach was necessary because, although a great number of articles, papers, and reports and even a book of conference presentations have been published about obsolescence, no book has been written specifically for managers or for practitioners who are responsible for dealing with the problem. My objective, therefore, was to fill this void. But unlike most of the published material on obsolescence, which is impressionistic and even simplistic in nature, the content of this book is to a large degree based on empirical evidence related to the multifaceted complexities of the problem. I have relied in part on my own investigations of obsolescence carried out over the past nine years, which have included in-depth interviews with managers, large-scale attitude surveys of professionals, and even long-range longitudinal research that has followed the same individuals from their first job after college through mid-career. The results of these investigations have been liberally sprinkled throughout the book. This information is being made available in an integrated fashion for the first time.

I have dwelt heavily on the three causes of obsolescence, namely, those which stem from (1) the information explosion and dynamic change stimulated by the knowledge revolution, (2) personal characteristics, particularly those which are psychological in nature, and (3) the work environment and organizational climate. It is first necessary to have a good understanding of why obsolescence occurs before it is possible to prescribe effective cures. The prescriptions I discuss focus on professional career development and involve a host of personnel practices and organizational changes, some widely accepted, others still new and untried. However, with the exception of continuing education, the suggested prescriptions have rarely been discussed in the context of obsolescence and certainly not in an integrated fashion.

Many individuals have contributed directly and indirectly along the long, tortuous, and frequently frustrating path leading to the development and publication of this book. My interest in the problem of obsolescence stems from the investigations I carried out under the guidance of R. Richard Ritti, whom I wish to acknowledge not only for his creative analyses of organizational professions, which appear primarily in Chapter 5, but also for his extremely helpful suggestions about the book in general. I also want to give special thanks to my colleagues Donald D. French, Edward D. Goldberg, Irwin Gray, and Larry Greenfield for providing very useful advice regarding some of the content as well as the style of the book. Among the others who have made contributions, I particularly want to single out Janyce Wolf, who went well beyond the call of duty as a reference librarian by persistently tracking down even the most obscure sources, and Carolyn Block, who helped transform my sometimes illegible handwriting into a readable manuscript. And finally, I wish to acknowledge the assistance rendered by the many individual managers from organizations that will have to remain anonymous, without whose cooperation my studies of obsolescence could not have been carried out.

H. G. KAUFMAN

CONTENTS

Chapter 1

The Challenge
of Change

ONE OF THE GREATEST CHALLENGES confronting all organizations is that of dynamic change. The effects of such change can be a threat not only to the organization's effectiveness but also to its very survival. In this chapter we will examine that change in order to see how it is related to the obsolescence of knowledge and skills among professionals. Among the most important factors that contribute to the turbulent flux in organizational environments are the following distinct but often interrelated types of change.[1]

1. *Technological change* is highly visible in the form of new products continually being created by new methods of production. Automation alone has revolutionized organizational processes ranging from record keeping to production control. One indication of this change is the staggering increase in the use of computers. The number of such machines grew from approximately 15 in the early fifties to 6,500 by 1960, passed 100,000 in 1970, and is expected to exceed 250,000 by the mid-seventies. Whether an organization prospers or perishes is often determined by the degree to which it utilizes technological innovations. Consequently, organizations have put increasing emphasis on technological forecasting to provide

direction to and stimulation of their research and development as well as their marketing efforts.

2. *Occupational change* is clearly evidenced by the fact that workers in white collar occupations with higher skill requirements now outnumber those in blue collar jobs, many of which are being eliminated as a result of increased mechanization, automation, and productivity. The most dramatic growth has been among managerial, professional, and technical personnel. These occupations, which accounted for only one-tenth of the labor force in 1950, today represent a quarter of the total working population. The number of professional personnel alone now exceeds the total of all skilled workers. Under the impact of technological change, new occupations with higher skill requirements are being created and old occupations are being changed, upgraded, or even eliminated. This occupational change is to a great extent made possible by the fact that almost a quarter of today's college-age population is completing bachelor and professional degrees, not to mention the burgeoning numbers of career-oriented junior-college graduates.

3. *Organizational change* is indicated by the fact that 66 percent of the largest American industrial corporations have reported recent major organizational changes exclusive of the restructuring that is always occurring at divisional and departmental levels. It has been estimated that large corporations now undergo at least one major reorganization every two years. Structural upheavals in organizations result from the mergers and acquisitions, diversification of products, expansion of international operations, and introduction of computers on a massive scale occurring in every sector of business and industry. Planned organizational change, ranging from the institution of new forms of project management to organization development programs designed to improve effectiveness at all levels of management, has become an integral part of corporate life.

4. *Change in managerial methods* is reflected in the widespread and increasing application of operations research and

systems analysis techniques, which emphasize quantitative and computer methodology to facilitate and improve management information, decision making, and forecasting. Management techniques also increasingly utilize behavioral science findings to improve motivation and productivity, as well as to enhance the development of the organization's human resources. The application of behavioral and management science techniques has become widespread in organizations only since the 1960s, and utilization of these methods continues to expand today and to affect every management function.

The preceding list is not exhaustive, and there are obviously additional types of related change that could be included. Among them are job and geographic mobility, new markets and marketing techniques, population growth and longer lifespan, increasing affluence, and a host of other social, economic, scientific, cultural, and political upheavals. The common denominator of many of these disparate types of change is dynamic growth. Yet growth itself is an end product of more fundamental but complex revolutionary changes that permeate today's society. Let us first examine the roots of that growth and then focus specifically on how growth has affected managerial, professional, and technical workers.

Emergence of a Knowledge Economy

Management and social analysts have attempted to identify and understand the factors that have contributed to the revolutionary changes that are occurring in organizational life as well as in society as a whole. There is apparent consensus that the dynamic growth of knowledge has had the greatest impact on the rapidly increasing introduction of new equipment and production techniques, new products, new occupations, and new methods of organization and management. The "knowledge revolution" has generally been attributed to the allocation of resources to research and development and educational activities, which together provide the basis for the production and distribution of new knowledge.

Funds for both R&D and education have increased at an exponential rate in the United States. For example, between 1776 and 1954, an estimated $40 billion was invested in R&D, whereas over $260 billion was allocated during the 16 years between 1955 and 1970. Although a leveling-off trend appeared in the late 1960s for both R&D and educational expenditures, the overall picture is nevertheless one of exponential growth whose rate of increase has exceeded that of the gross national product (GNP). Viewed in another way, expenditures for R&D and education together accounted for approximately 5 percent of the GNP during the early fifties, but by the late sixties the figure had already doubled to a level of 10 percent.[2]

The knowledge revolution has drastically altered the mix of industries in the United States and has brought us closer to what has been termed a "knowledge economy." [3] The growth of the "knowledge industries," which deal with the production and distribution of ideas and information rather than goods and services, has been nothing less than phenomenal.[4] The knowledge industries include all aspects of education, R&D, communications media, and information production and dissemination. The "knowledge sector" of the U.S. economy grew to one-quarter of the GNP by 1955, a threefold increase from 1900, and continued to grow to one-third of the GNP by 1965. Given projections that knowledge production and distribution will reach one-half of the GNP by the late 1970s, it is apparent that, within the lifetime of a generation, the United States will have been transformed from a goods-producing economy into a knowledge economy.

Professionalization of the Workforce

The change in the industrial mix toward a knowledge economy has created a need for manpower that possesses high levels of knowledge and skills. The result has been an increased professionalization of the workforce.[5] The proportion of all workers employed in knowledge industries has grown from one out of ten in 1900 to one out of three in 1959. As this trend continues, workers in knowledge industries should form the majority of the American labor force by the late 1970s.[6] Many of the "knowledge workers" are highly educated, and they have created a workforce whose expectations are different from those of unskilled or blue collar workers. The change in the composition of the workforce has in turn necessitated changes in methods of personnel management and organization.

The emergence of a workforce of organizational professionals, although largely stimulated by knowledge industry growth, has occurred in all sectors of the American economy. Occupations are generally classified as professional if they require a base of specialized intellectual and practical knowledge acquired through education and experience. Organizational professionals, who pursue careers in a variety of occupations in business, industry, and government, have been and will continue to be the fastest growing segment of the labor force. Some of those occupations are listed in Table 1, together with an estimate of the number employed in each occupation as of 1970 and the projected annual growth rate to 1980. These occupational groups contribute directly through their respective activities to organizational survival and success; indeed, organizations could no longer exist without them. Given their importance, we should take a closer look at these professional occupations, which for convenience have been classified into four major groups.

SALARIED MANAGERS

The number of salaried managers working in business, industry, and government increased by almost 80 percent between 1960 and 1970 and is growing at the astounding average rate of over 260,000 per year. Salaried managers comprise the single largest and one of the fastest growing of all occupational groups. (Managers are classified as professionals because management positions in organizations generally require some specialized intellectual and practical knowledge acquired by means of education and experience, and henceforth the term "professionals" will apply to salaried managers also.) It is very likely that a high rate of growth in the number of salaried managers will continue into the immediate future.

TABLE 1   Employment of selected organizational professionals in 1970 and projections of average annual openings to 1980.

OCCUPATIONAL CLASSIFICATION	ESTIMATED EMPLOYMENT IN 1970	ESTIMATED AVERAGE ANNUAL OPENINGS TO 1980
Salaried managers	6,000,000	270,000
Technical professionals		
Engineers	1,100,000	53,000
Physical scientists	250,000	12,900
Life scientists	191,000	10,700
Mathematicians	100,000	6,400
Natural scientists	42,000	1,800
Total	1,683,000	84,800
Business professionals		
Accountants	500,000	31,200
Personnel specialists	160,000	9,100
Advertising specialists	141,000	8,400
Public relations specialists	78,000	4,400
Economists	33,000	2,300
Marketing researchers	23,000	2,600
Total	935,000	58,000
Computer professionals		
Programmers	200,000	23,000
Systems analysts	100,000	22,700
Total	300,000	45,700

SOURCE: *Occupational Outlook Handbook*, 1972–1973 ed. Bureau of Labor Statistics Bulletin 1700; *Occupational Outlook Quarterly*, Vol. 14 (1970), No. 2, pp. 7–12; *New York Times*, September 25, 1972, p. 32.

During the 1970s, a shortage in the 35–44-year age group should result in openings at middle management levels. These openings will have to be filled by tapping the enormous pool of candidates in the 25–34-year age group. Those in this early career stage will comprise one out of every four workers in the labor force, and over a third of them will have completed some college education. This will result in an unprecedented number of young organizational professionals being available as candidates for advancement into middle management. Since most of those selected from that group will have completed some higher education, the process of professionalization of management will be further accelerated. The professionalization process is almost complete at the highest levels of organizations; practically every executive has had a college education.[7] Selection for middle management, as well as for entry-level management positions, is becoming increasingly dependent on the prospective candidate's education and functional specialization. These criteria for selection have served to create a more knowledge-oriented managerial workforce.

TECHNICAL PROFESSIONALS

Engineers, scientists, and mathematicians comprise the technical professional group, which—among professionals in American business and industry—is second in size only to managers. The work of the technical professionals has been directly responsible for the knowledge explosion. According to National Science Foundation statistics, the number of engineers and scientists almost doubled in the decade between 1950 and 1960.[8] The numbers continued to grow during the next decade, so that by 1970 there were almost 1.7 million technical professionals, or one out of every fifty workers in the American labor force. Despite the large-scale layoffs of engineers and scientists following the defense, aerospace, and R&D cutbacks beginning in 1969, shortages of engineers and some scientists by 1980 are projected.

The anticipated shortages of engineers and scientists may be attributable to the decline in enrollment in engineering and science curricula, as well as to the fact that the temporary unavailability and insecurity of jobs in their fields has prompted many technical professionals to seek employment outside their areas. The average annual number of openings for engineers alone is estimated at 53,000 per year during the 1970s, and requirements for an engineering workforce of 1.5 million are projected for 1980. Among physical scientists, chemists are projected to be most in demand, and 200,000 are expected to be needed by 1980. Physicists may also be in somewhat short supply; an estimated 75,000 will be required by 1980, despite the surplus of such scientists during the early 1970s. The growth in number of engineers and scientists will result in a technical workforce of well over 2 million by 1980. The phenomenal recent increase in the numbers of such professionals is reflected in the estimate that 90 percent of all the engineers and scientists who ever lived are alive and working today.

One of the consequences of its rapid emergence is that the large technical workforce now provides a major manpower pool from which managers are selected. According to several studies, over half of America's chief executives in nonfinancial corporations may be coming from the ranks of engineers and scientists as compared with only 7 percent at the turn of the century.[9] The reason is not only that large numbers of technical professionals work in organizations but also that important managerial decisions today often require technical and other specialized knowledge and the practical problem-solving orientation of most engineers and many scientists. Consequently, technical professionals have drastically changed the composition of managerial manpower. They are bringing their professional expertise to even the highest levels of corporate management, and they are thereby further reinforcing the emphasis on the creation and utilization of new knowledge.

BUSINESS PROFESSIONALS

The business professionals include such diverse groups as accountants, personnel and advertising specialists, economists, and marketing researchers. In 1970, these business specialists comprised a workforce of approximately one million. The largest single group of business specialists are the half million accountants, approximately three-fourths of whom work in management accounting within business, industry, or government. Accounting employment is expected to expand very rapidly during the 1970s. The 31,200 average openings per year will result in a need for approximately three-quarters of a million accountants by 1980. Rapid expansion during the 1970s in the numbers of college-educated employees working in such specialties as marketing research, public relations, and personnel is also projected.

The growth in the number of business specialists has provided another source of management manpower. Although technical professionals tend to fill many of the top corporate executive positions, business specialists also are found at the highest organizational levels. Among the largest industrial, merchandising, and transportation companies in the United States, 13 percent of the chief executives have degrees in accounting.[10] In addition, 5 percent of those executives have an academic background in economics and another 5 percent in marketing. However, when other executive positions are examined, approximately 80 percent of the controllers, 61 percent of the treasurers, and 56 percent of the financial vice presidents are found to have an accounting education. Moreover, some 14 percent of the financial vice presidents and 13 percent of the treasurers have degrees in economics. The growth and increasingly important role of various business specialties bring a diversity of knowledge to the operations of organizations and thereby stimulate change not only in the functional staff areas but also at the highest levels of management.

COMPUTER PROFESSIONALS

Some 200,000 programmers and over 100,000 systems analysts are included in the computer professional group. In view of the fact that this specialist group hardly existed in 1950, its spectacular expansion ranks it as the fastest growing of the organizational professional groups.

The growth rate in the number of programmers and systems analysts during the 1970s will continue to be rapid. Almost 46,000 openings will be created each year, and that will result in a projected workforce of a million computer professionals by the early 1980s. Naturally, the growth rate reflects the fact that the operations of modern organizations are becoming increasingly dependent on electronic data processing and computer professionals. Owing to the recent origins of their occupation, computer professionals generally have a background in another specialty such as engineering, mathematics, or accounting. Another recent phenomenon is the entry into higher levels of management by systems analysts, which is likely to increase greatly in the immediate future.[11] The rapid expansion of computer technology and expertise into all phases of organizational life will assure continuing changes not only in manpower and skill requirements but in organizational structure and management methods as well.

The Information Explosion

The rapid increase in the number of knowledge workers has resulted in a staggering growth in the production and distribution of new information that is often referred to as the information explosion.[12] The dynamic growth is reflected in the overwhelming proliferation of books, journals, abstracts, reports, papers, and patents. Information is considered to be the communication of knowledge. Hence, all information can be classified as knowledge but not all knowledge can be called information for the reason that some knowledge has not been communicated via information channels.

The information explosion is perhaps most evident to scientists. The number of scientific journals alone has increased at an exponential rate; it has doubled every 15 years since the birth of such journals over 300 years ago.[13] By the middle of the nineteenth century, the number of scientific journals was such that the information needs of specialists were met by abstract journals, which then started to increase in number at the same rate as that of the journals. Abstract journals appeared when the number of scientific journals reached the critical number of 300. By the middle of the twentieth century the number of abstract journals had reached the critical level of 300, which necessitated the use of computer abstracting for information retrieval. If the growth in number of scientific journals continues at its present rate, a staggering 1 million such journals will be published by the year 2000.

The flood of literature has affected all organizational professionals, although the information explosion is more pronounced in some disciplines than in others. From an examination of the recent growth rate in new professional books in business, science, and technology (see Table 2), it is clear that the rates of increase between 1960 and 1970 have surpassed the growth rates of the preceding decade. Although the absolute number of new books in business is still less than in science or technology, the present growth rate is highest among business books. These figures may in fact be understating the changes, since if all new books relevant to business are included, well over 3,000 are now appearing annually.

TABLE 2   New books and new editions published in the United States during 1950, 1960, and 1970.

				PERCENT INCREASE	
SUBJECT	1950	1960	1970	1950–1960	1960–1970
Business	250	305	797	22.0	123.9
Science	705	1,089	2,358	54.5	116.5
Technology	497	698	1,141	40.4	63.5
All subjects	11,022	15,012	36,071	36.2	140.3

SOURCE: *Statistical Abstracts of the United States,* 1970, and *Publishers Weekly,* February 8, 1971.

The information explosion in business media is reflected by the increasing growth rates of new journals in practically every area relevant to management. The most dramatic change has occurred in the computer and operations research areas, in which an average of 14 new journals appeared annually between 1960 and 1970 compared with only 3 per year during the preceding decade. Even in such long-established business specialties as accounting, in which the growth in the number of journals had remained relatively constant in recent decades, there has been a dramatic exponential growth in the common body of knowledge (see Figure 1). A conservative estimate indicates that approximately 2,500 different periodicals relevant to business and management are published each year in the United States. Given this accelerating growth rate of published knowledge, the information explosion appears to be affecting management and business professions today very much as it affected science and technology previously.

That the accelerating growth of new information and ideas has continued unabated in science and technology is partially reflected in the issuance of patents. Since the end of World War II, the total number of patents issued in the United States has been approximately doubling every decade. Over 70,000 new patents appeared annually by the beginning of the 1970s, and rates went as high as 3,275 new patents per day. The dynamic increase in patents clearly presents a challenge to those who are responsible for creating products or production innovations that keep their organizations viable and competitive.

The retrieval of information has become much more complex with the proliferation of less accessible publications in the form of government research reports, corporate house organs, and institutional research papers. The U.S. government alone publishes an estimated 100,000 reports annually in addition to 450,000 papers, articles, and books. American business and industry regularly publish over 1,000 corporate journals. An incalculable number of papers are produced by the academically based research institutes in the United States, which

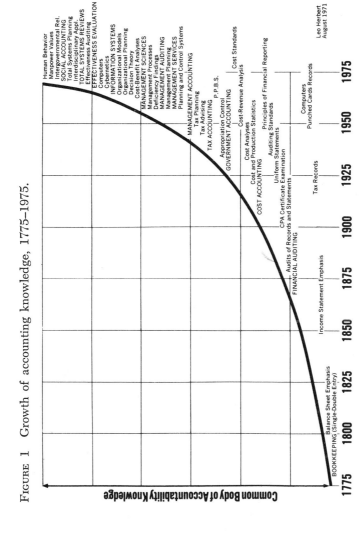

FIGURE 1 Growth of accounting knowledge, 1775–1975.

SOURCE: W. N. Conrardy, "Accounting Education: For What Purpose?" Reprinted with permission from the Winter 1972 issue of *The Journal of Contemporary Business*, University of Washington.

number more than 4,500, or almost four times the number in 1960. As a result of its inaccessibility, it is very likely that most organizational professionals will never be exposed to much of this information.

The Problem of Information Acquisition

If organizational professionals are to keep up to date with the continually increasing deluge of information in their fields, it would appear necessary that they devote a considerable amount of time to reading about new developments.[14] For example, the annual output in chemistry is approximately a quarter of a million books, articles, and papers. Consequently, chemists would have to spend an impossible amount of time reading about current developments in their profession. However, a carefully carried out nationwide study revealed that, on the average, chemists spend only two hours per week reading scientific journals. The study further indicated that any one chemist reads only about one half of one percent of the articles published in chemistry.

This situation is not peculiar to chemists, since physicists also were found to spend two hours per week reading the current literature. Other studies corroborate these findings; all report that engineers and scientists spend an average of less than three hours per week reading technical periodicals. Even the few hours of reading that technical professionals do manage are primarily devoted to specific job needs and not to updating. An investigation of the information utilized by several thousand engineers and scientists reveals that well under half of the time spent in reading professional journals, books, and papers is devoted to maintaining general competence by reviewing new developments, brushing up in a field, or trying to learn about a new field. Consequently, the average time scientists and engineers spend on keeping up to date with the professional literature is only *one hour per week*. As we shall see in Chapter 5, the demands of the work itself can influence the effort devoted to reading the current literature.

At this point, suffice it to say that certain types of work pressure cause the majority of professionals to feel that they have insufficient time for reading during working hours. The problem is particularly acute among those in technical management. The lack of time for reading is felt by management of all types and on all levels. Executives universally complain that they have insufficient time for reading the current literature and that what little time they do have must be found at home during their leisure hours. Although studies have indicated that middle managers allocate an average of 10 percent of their total time at work to reading, their reading is more closely connected with the immediate demands of their jobs than with keeping up to date with new developments generally. Among first-level industrial managers, more than three out of four feel it is important to read and to use the library to obtain information, yet approximately half of them seldom or never actually engage in these activities. Indications are that only one out of five first-line supervisors and one out of four middle-level managers make frequent use of management journals.

To keep abreast of new published information, it has been estimated that 20 percent of a professional's working time should be devoted to reading.[15] Yet it is quite apparent that, in spite of the information explosion, organizational professionals are not spending an adequate amount of time in keeping current with new developments, at least by means of reading the current literature. Even more disturbing is that, among technical professionals and specialized managers, the major source of information for keeping up to date is the published literature.[16] The implications are clear: *few organizational professionals are keeping abreast of new knowledge in their fields.*

This problem has come to the attention of managers, educators, and social scientists. Typical of the general conclusions reached by most of the analysts is the following one by T. Keith Glennan, who, as president of Case Institute of Technology, played a significant role in revamping the education of technical professionals in response to the rapid changes that occurred after World War II:

> The rising tide of new knowledge will bring unprecedented opportunities, but it will bring unprecedented problems as well. One problem will be the rapid obsolescence of machines and processes; but far more serious will be the threat of obsolescence of men at every level. . . . *Within a decade, the obsolescence of skilled, technical, and scientific manpower will be recognized as industry's most pressing problem.*[17]

This prediction was made in 1965, and professional manpower obsolescence should therefore already have become a critical problem. The objectives of this book are to determine to what degree this is true, to examine the causes of obsolescence, and to prescribe immediate and long-range cures before the problem becomes unmanageable. American corporations are already feeling the effects of product competition from knowledge-based industries overseas, and some countries have surpassed the United States in certain areas of technology. Business and industry must protect their considerable investment in professional manpower and deal with the problem of obsolescence, since it is clear that what may be at stake is survival in an environment of increasing change and competition.

THE ROOTS of obsolescence have been traced to the knowledge revolution, the information explosion, and the dynamic changes that have occurred in technology, occupations, organizational structure, and management methods. The movement toward a knowledge economy that produces and distributes ideas and information requires manpower with high levels of knowledge and skills and, thereby, increases the professionalization of the workforce.

Professionals generally require a base of specialized and practical knowledge acquired through education and experience. The largest professional groups in business, industrial, and governmental organizations are those of salaried managers and technical specialists. Smaller numbers of professionals are employed in a variety of business areas or as computer specialists.

All these groups are increasing in number at a rapid rate. The technical professionals have made the greatest impact not only because of their numerical strength and their entry in large numbers into management positions but also because of their having been primarily responsible for the knowledge explosion and its effects. Consequently, problems such as information acquisition have been of greater concern to technical professionals than to other groups. They nevertheless spend an inadequate amount of time keeping abreast of the literature in their fields, which makes them prime candidates for obsolescence. It should, however, be obvious that obsolescence is much more complex than just reading to keep up to date.

In the remaining chapters, the insights gained from disparate research as well as from practical experience have been integrated to provide managers and practitioners with an understanding of obsolescence in order to bring the problem under organizational control. Chapter 2 examines the meaning of obsolescence, the extent of the problem among different professional groups, and the difficult question of how to detect and measure obsolescence in organizations. Chapter 3 evaluates the widespread assumption that obsolescence inevitably increases with age, and focuses on the psychological factors which affect obsolescence during the career. Chapter 4 demonstrates how individual differences among professionals may have utility in personnel practices that deal with selection and placement, assessment, counseling, and retirement.

The effects of the work environment on obsolescence are explored in Chapter 5, which focuses on the problems of work challenge and the utilization of knowledge and skills. Job design and enrichment are discussed as techniques that are applicable to combatting obsolescence. Chapter 6 explores how the organizational climate affects professional obsolescence and discusses the role of colleague interaction and communication, supervisory style and expertise, and management policies in discouraging obsolescence. The use of reward systems such as the dual ladder of advancement and organizational change and development complete the discussion of climate.

In Chapter 7 continuing education and the differential effects of various methods used for keeping professionals up to date are explored. Finally, Chapter 8 presents a concise summary of the conclusions reached and the prescriptions advocated in the preceding chapters and provides guidelines for management to follow in stimulating professional development to control obsolescence. The need for a greater understanding of the causes and cures of obsolescence is highlighted in a discussion of how business and industry can integrate their interests with those of the professional societies, educational institutions, and the federal government in a center for obsolescence research.

Chapter 2

Obsolescence:
Its Definition, Scope,
and Measurement

OBSOLESCENT PROFESSIONALS can have debilitating effects on organizational effectiveness and efficiency in terms of both human and monetary costs. Obsolescence can ultimately be manifested by a variety of symptoms that may include low job satisfaction and morale, decreased productivity, limited advancement opportunities, increased turnover, increased hiring, higher salary costs, increased competition, and limited growth. Given the gravity of these problems, it is not surprising that obsolescence among organizational professionals has become a widely discussed management issue. What may be surprising, however, is that, despite the widespread concern, it is one of the most poorly understood of the organization's human problems. Yet management decisions about manpower allocations and development are continually being made in the guise of combatting obsolescence. They often involve the expenditure of significant financial resources, particularly for updating activities.

Concern about the obsolescence of organizational professionals has kept pace with accelerating change and the proliferation of knowledge. By the early 1960s the issue had come to be of heightened interest to management. Concern over this issue continued to grow so rapidly that, within less than a decade, hundreds of articles and papers had been written and at least half a dozen national or international conferences and symposia had focused on the issue of obsolescence and updating. Although such activities are indicative of the energy being directed toward understanding and dealing with obsolescence, much of the literature and discussion has remained at an impressionistic and speculative level, and the few research studies have been largely descriptive. Nevertheless, these efforts allow us to see how obsolescence has been defined, how widespread it is as a problem, and how it can be detected or measured.

Defining Obsolescence

One of the first problems encountered in a discussion of the obsolescence of organizational professionals is finding a definition of the concept that is unambiguous and universally acceptable. The problem is epitomized by the fact that the behavioral scientists, including personnel researchers from major U.S. corporations, who participated in the First Conference on Occupational Obsolescence convened in 1966 were unable to arrive at a clear-cut definition that was acceptable to all.[1]

Organizational researchers who have investigated obsolescence more recently also have lacked unanimity in their definitions. One of the peculiarities that emerges when obsolescence definitions are examined is that the concept is usually discussed as either technical or managerial obsolescence. For the sake of conciseness, one definition that applies to both technical and managerial obsolescence would be desirable. By integrating the dimensions common to the definitions used in a variety of studies,[2] three characteristics were identified.

A LACK OF NEW KNOWLEDGE OR SKILLS

All definitions of obsolescence, regardless of whether they deal with technical or managerial manpower, agree on at least one factor: *obsolescence occurs when the individual lacks new knowledge or skills.* Additional support for that comes from a National Science Foundation study of continuing education that also focused on a deficiency dimension and stated unequivocally that "obsolescence must always be a function of new knowledge and techniques." [3] The unanimity leaves little doubt that obsolescence necessarily involves a failure on the part of the professional to keep up to date with knowledge or skills. However, there are varying degrees of obsolescence; no professional is ever completely up to date, and few are totally obsolete. Questions that still remain are what consequences the lack of new knowledge and skills has for the organizational professional and how these consequences relate to a concept of obsolescence.

INEFFECTIVENESS

Almost every definition of obsolescence ties the concept to ineffectiveness. However, not every type of ineffectiveness should be attributed to obsolescence. For example, a professional who has the most up-to-date knowledge and skills but is unwilling or unable to use them may be ineffective but not obsolescent. His ineffectiveness may be attributable to personal or organizational factors that inhibit the use of knowledge and skills. Only ineffectiveness that stems directly from a lack of awareness of current knowledge and skills should be attributed to obsolescence. Although that type of ineffectiveness is clearly part of the obsolescence concept, it may be more relevant to some work roles than to others.

JOB AND PROFESSIONAL ROLES

Practically all definitions of obsolescence connect the concept to the individual's performance in his current organizational work role. Consequently, professionals who lack the knowledge or skills necessary to perform their current jobs effectively are obsolescent. This has sometimes been referred to as *job assignment obsolescence.*

However, other types of obsolescence relevant to specialist or professional career roles have also been identified, although with less frequency than the job assignment type. Those roles may be affected by *professional obsolescence,* which occurs when individuals do not keep up with the latest developments in their disciplines. Such obsolescence potentially impairs effectiveness of performance in future work roles during the professional career. For this reason, professional obsolescence is similar to what has sometimes been referred to as *versatility* or *potential obsolescence.* Although individuals may be up to date in their present job assignments, they may not have kept current in their professional areas, and so their capability to take on different or greater responsibilities is limited. This type of professional obsolescence has perhaps been most visible among technical professionals in the aerospace industry who were laid off. These individuals were up to date in the specialized knowledge and skills required by their jobs, but they had failed to maintain a professional versatility that would have facilitated their reemployment in another industry.

Deterioration is not obsolescence. There is very limited support for a definition of obsolescence that involves a *loss* rather than a *lack* of certain capabilities. For example, one definition has identified a loss of previously acquired knowledge as an aspect of technical obsolescence. Similarly, other definitions that involve managerial obsolescence have pointed to a loss of motivation, physical stamina, or capacity to adapt to change. These losses in knowledge or individual strengths are more properly defined as *deterioration* than as obsolescence. As will be evident in the next chapter, they are the types of individual characteristics that may contribute to obsolescence. Consequently, managers should avoid confusing the concept of obsolescence with the personal weaknesses that may be its causes. It should be noted, however, that since a reduction in performance effectiveness may be a result but not a cause of obsolescence, a performance decrement can be included in the concept.

A SYNTHESIZED CONCEPT OF OBSOLESCENCE

The dimensions that have been identified as part of a concept of obsolescence among organizational professionals may be integrated to form a general definition: *Obsolescence is the degree to which organizational professionals lack the up-to-date knowledge or skills necessary to maintain effective performance in either their current or future work roles.*

How Widespread Is Obsolescence?

Since the rate of increase in new knowledge and skills is not the same for different professional groups, it would be expected that the degree to which obsolescence is a problem also would depend on the individual's professional group membership. Although only a handful of relevant descriptive studies exist, it would nevertheless be useful to examine them to determine the extent to which obsolescence is a problem among various organizational professions.

TECHNICAL PROFESSIONALS

As a result of rapid technological change, the problem of obsolescence appears to be most pronounced among engineers and scientists, who, paradoxically, are often responsible for creating such change.[4] A survey among 39 firms revealed that almost all (89 percent) regard obsolescence of their technical professionals to be a problem and seven out of ten companies find it a major or sizable one. That technical professionals may in fact be most affected by technological change is revealed in studies of nonsupervisory engineers, who most frequently point to the threat of obsolescence as the greatest problem facing them during the 1970s. Almost all of those engineers (95 percent) feel that technical obsolescence is a problem. One out of four identify it as serious, and nine out of ten indicate it will become even more difficult to deal with in the future. Another study, which included scientists as well as engineers, also reveals that almost all (89 percent) feel that keeping up with technological developments is a problem, and 36 percent feel that the problem is serious. Although technical professionals are almost unanimous in feeling that keeping up to date is a problem, the question that remains is how many are actually obsolescent. A report by Stanford Research Institute provides conservative estimates that job assignment obsolescence seriously affects at least one in five engineers but only one out of fifteen scientists. The report also estimates that professional obsolescence seriously affects more than half of all engineers and at least a quarter of all scientists. Based on these estimates, it is projected that more than 600,000 engineers and 125,000 scientists in the United States may experience difficulty in taking on new assignments within their professional fields.

Some of these disconcerting estimates tend to be supported by other research studies. Two independent investigations of large samples of engineers found that approximately half are unaware of most of the emerging knowledge in engineering. Furthermore, pure researchers have been found to be most up to date among the technical professionals and production engineers to be most obsolescent. The reasons for such differences in obsolescence levels between engineers and scientists, as well as among functional areas, are associated with organizational as well as professional roles. It is rather clear, however, that the overwhelming majority of technical professionals perceive obsolescence to be a real and continuing threat and that perhaps as many as half of them are already affected by the problem.

SALARIED MANAGERS

A survey of 64 companies that represent a wide range of industries and are recognized leaders in their fields reveals that managerial obsolescence is currently or potentially a problem in three out of four of the organizations.[5] Furthermore, some 65 percent of the executives questioned in the study project that managerial obsolescence will continue to be a problem during the 1970s and indicate that the consequences could be serious unless companies update their managers. There is an expectation among the organizations that new management techniques will continue to be developed and will become more widespread in use. In fact, technological change and obsolescence are already a major cause of managerial layoffs and, according to one report, account for 44 percent of the managers being dismissed.

As is true of technical professionals, the degree to which obsolescence is a problem among managers is at least in part determined by their functional area. For example, managers in engineering appear to be the most threatened by obsolescence; most of them (86 percent) consider it a problem, and one out of four describe it as serious. In fact, technical managers are more likely than nonsupervisory engineers to report that keeping up to date is the most serious problem facing them in the 1970s, and they feel it will become increasingly harder to deal with in the future. This tends to be supported by a large-scale study of managers in 44 technically oriented companies. Most of the managers considered their training and experience to be sufficient for their current jobs, but 71 percent anticipated inadequacies in the next two to five years. Managers of technical professionals have an especially acute problem because they are subject to obsolescence not only in management methods but in their technical specialties as well.

The dual problem of obsolescence among managers is not as extreme in functions other than technical management, but it nevertheless exists to varying degrees. A study of computer marketing managers indicates that only a minority (38 percent) feel that obsolescence is at least a fairly serious problem. That is very likely due to the fact that almost all (89 percent) indicate that a general business knowledge is more important to their performance than knowledge about computers or data processing.

In an investigation of managerial obsolescence in advertising agencies, three out of four executives report that their agencies have such a problem, but generally they do not think it is serious. Over half of the agencies indicate that between 10 and 25 percent of their managerial staff are affected by obsolescence. However, even among advertising managers it is generally felt that the problem of obsolescence applies more to those in specialized functional areas such as account management.

A study of personnel executives reveals that eight out of ten are unaware of 30 percent or more of the knowledge relevant to their function. Despite the fact that a knowledge score of 50 percent could have been attained purely by guessing, over 15 percent of the executives failed to reach even that level. Consequently, the 15 percent figure may represent a conservative estimate of professional obsolescence among personnel executives. If this percentage is applied to all managers, there may be one million experiencing managerial obsolescence.

The propensity of managers to become obsolescent is affected not only by functional area but also by level in the organization's hierarchy. Executives at higher levels are reported to have the greatest need to stay abreast of new management concepts and techniques so they will be able to guide lower-level managers. However, obsolescence of technical knowledge and skills is much more of a problem to lower-level managers, who are in more direct contact with the organizational specialists with whom they must be able to communicate.

Although obsolescence does not appear to be as widespread among managers as it is among technical professionals, the problem may be more serious for those who manage specialized functions. What is clear is that managerial obsolescence threatens most organizations and may soon become as widespread a problem as technical obsolescence.

OTHER ORGANIZATIONAL PROFESSIONALS

What about the obsolescence of organizational professionals other than technical specialists or managers? There is an extreme paucity of information on professionals in business and computer specialties.[6] That may be due to the fact that technological change and the information explosion have had a greater impact on much larger numbers of managers and technical specialists than on other organizational professionals. Of course, that does not mean that the other professionals have not been affected by accelerated change. In fact, five out of six corporations report that obsolescence among many kinds of professional personnel will become a general problem during the 1970s and the limited data that do exist indicate that it is already happening. For instance, obsolescence is reported as a fairly serious problem among 44 percent of computer marketing personnel and among 48 percent of other data processing professionals. Although these figures are considerably below the level of obsolescence among technical professionals, the knowledge explosion is likely to have an impact on other specialties in the next generation similar to that experienced by science and technology in the current generation.

Now that we have formulated a definition of obsolescence and have a general idea of who is affected and to what extent, let us turn to the question that is constantly posed: How does one measure obsolescence?

Measuring Obsolescence in the Organization

Obviously the greater the percentage of obsolescent professionals in an organization, the higher the likelihood that the organization itself will become obsolete. Organizational obsolescence may be viewed as the degree to which professional and highly skilled personnel have failed to keep up to date with the knowledge and skills necessary for effective current or future organizational performance. Organizations can become obsolete if their various functions (research, development, production, marketing, sales, accounting, personnel), as well as general management, utilize methods that are outdated and not as effective as those that are currently available and may be employed by competing firms. Managers can detect obsolescence by examining their organization's performance and attempting to answer such questions as these:

- Have products changed little or not at all over a long period of time?
- Have few new methods been introduced?
- Have few new ideas been developed?
- Have errors in decision making increased?
- Has there been an increase in the effectiveness of competition?
- Has output been on the conservative side?

If the answer to some of these questions is affirmative, the organization may very well be obsolescent and possibly on its way to joining the thousands of business failures that occur annually in the United States. However, by the time the symptoms and consequences of obsolescence are detected, it may already be too late to save the organization.

To avoid arriving at a state in which organizational survival is threatened, management should periodically monitor the degree to which its professional manpower is obsolescent. What is required is some method of measuring obsolescence. Unfortunately, there are no simple direct measures, but many relatively accessible indices have been used to reflect obsolescence indirectly. There are also measures that may be more direct but are also more difficult to obtain. The often expressed desire of managers and personnel researchers to have some measure of obsolescence may be satisfied, at least to some extent, by approaching the problem of measurement on two not necessarily mutually exclusive levels: (1) the macro level, which is concerned with indices of obsolescence on an organizationwide basis, and (2) the micro level, which is concerned with determining to what degree the individual professional is obsolescent. In order to measure obsolescence on any level, two general methods can be applied. They involve either (1) an analysis of information accessible from personnel record data or (2) the use of more complicated techniques involving organizational analyses. Let us now examine in detail how these two methods may provide measures of obsolescence.

PERSONNEL RECORD DATA

Organizations can tap personnel records, which may exist as part of a computerized personnel data system, to get information about age, education, performance, skills, and professional contributions. Such data have been utilized to measure the extent of obsolescence in the organization. Some of the information from personnel records has also been used to detect individual obsolescence, although it is clear that most of the indices do not conform to the definition of obsolescence presented earlier.

1. *Age.* One very broad index is the age distribution of an organization's professionals. Although the association of age and obsolescence is controversial, as we shall see in Chapter 3, it has nevertheless been used to provide a rough but usually accessible index of organizational obsolescence. An organization that is top-heavy with older professionals may be on its way to becoming obsolescent if it has not already become so. However, age by itself should not be used as an indicator of individual obsolescence, since it tells us nothing about the knowledge and skills or effectiveness of the professional.

2. *Education and training.* Some indices, which are somewhat more relevant to the concept of obsolescence than age, utilize records of education and training activities of the professionals in the organization. Such indices have ranged from a simple degree count by major and year received to tabulations of number and type of courses completed most recently. Organizations with an appreciable number of professionals who have not participated in any education or training for many years may be very prone to obsolescence.

Updating activities have been so central to dealing with obsolescence that they are extensively discussed in later chapters. At this point suffice it to say that some record of updating activities may be utilized as an indirect index of organizational as well as individual obsolescence. However, gradu-

ate-level education is generally relevant to professional obsolescence, whereas training is usually more relevant to job
assignment obsolescence. In both cases the connection with the
definition of obsolescence is still tenuous, since neither implies
effectiveness in job or profession.

3. *Performance rating.* Performance ratings have been widely
used as measures of obsolescence. One approach is to use a
static distribution of the current performance ratings among
professionals as a macro index of organizational obsolescence.
If there is a relatively high percent of mediocre or below-
average professionals, their ineffectiveness may be a result, at
least in part, of obsolescence.

A more relevant index of organizational obsolescence can be
obtained by utilizing a dynamic measure involving the change
in the distribution of performance ratings over time. A decrement in the performance of professionals as indicated by a
smaller percent of high performers as compared with a prior
period may be a consequence of obsolescence. Performance
rating data when applied to graphic techniques such as management inventory charts (see Figure 2), can provide an audit
of individual obsolescence. However, as has already been
noted, not all types of performance ineffectiveness are associated with obsolescence. Only by an appraisal of the individual professional can it be ascertained that poor performance
is a result of obsolescence, and performance ratings are therefore not totally adequate even for measuring job assignment
obsolescence. Methods of performance appraisal can, however,
be used to detect individual obsolescence, and they are described in Chapter 4.

4. *Professional contributions and activities.* Personnel records
often contain information on professional contributions and
activities that indicate the degree to which the individual
keeps up with and contributes to new knowledge. Typical
records have information on patents, publications, papers presented at meetings, and participation in professional societies.
Organizations can identify the activities that are most related

to the various professional functions. For example, patent contributions are most relevant to technical professionals in R&D. Any index developed by using personnel records is more likely to be relevant to professional than job assignment obsolescence. Note that although professional contributions may come

FIGURE 2   Management inventory chart.

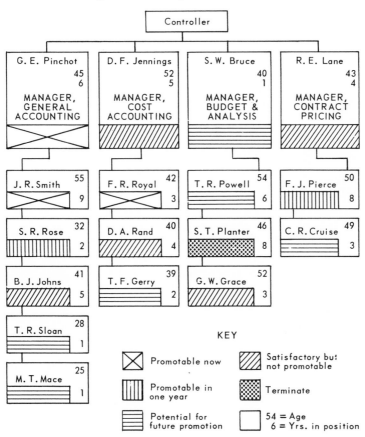

SOURCE: From *Principles of Management* by H. A. Koontz and C. O'Donnell. Used with permission of McGraw-Hill Book Company, copyright 1964.

from individuals who are up to date, those who do not make such contributions are not necessarily obsolescent.

5. *Skills inventories.* Many organizations keep skills inventories in the personnel records of their professionals, usually as part of a computerized personnel data system. Typically, the original information for skills inventories is obtained by having the professionals select, from a coded list, the specialties in which they are proficient and the last year of use for each specialty. Some problems have arisen from the use of very extensive and lengthy skills records obtained from inventories. A more effective approach would be to limit the maximum number of specialties to a more manageable and perhaps more meaningful number. The records of individuals must be updated periodically, as must the list of skills in the inventory itself. From such records, the knowledge and skills currently available in the organization can be ascertained. This can provide information for measuring job assignment, as well as professional obsolescence, of both individuals and the organization as a whole. However, possession of knowledge and skills does not always mean that the professional can apply them effectively.

As should be obvious, all of the preceding methods have inherent weaknesses as measures of obsolescence, particularly with respect to individual measurement. Although most of the information is available from personnel records, it can be easily argued that characteristics retrieved from files really may not measure obsolescence as it has been defined. All that is suggested is that information which is readily available in personnel files can be used as a gross indicator of the degree to which obsolescence may exist in the organization. More direct, sophisticated, and costly techniques can be developed by using various methods that have been broadly classified under organizational analyses.

ORGANIZATIONAL ANALYSES

As used here, the term "organizational analysis" refers broadly to any approach used to measure the strengths and weaknesses, as reported by members of an organization, that could influence effectiveness. The approaches that can be used to obtain more direct measures of obsolescence include attitude surveys, knowledge ratings, and knowledge tests.

Attitude surveys. Many organizations utilize job-related attitude or opinion surveys of their employees for various purposes that can range from identifying and analyzing particular problems to carrying out extensive organizational change and development. Such surveys can easily include questions relevant to the measurement of obsolescence in the organization. The questions may take several forms. Professionals may be asked directly how up to date they are in general, as in the following example from a survey of the professional and technical personnel of a major corporation:

Do you feel that you have been able to keep up to date with recent technical developments in your field of specialty?

1   I am completely up to date.
2   Pretty well up to date.
3   Only fairly well up to date.
4   I am not at all up to date.

The preceding question asks the professional to express his perception of his own obsolescence. Obviously, he may be unwilling or unable to do so. To avoid that bias, the question can focus on professionals in general rather than on the individual, as in the following example from the same questionnaire:

In your opinion is there any significant problem in your area created by the fact that professionals have not kept up with new developments in their field?

1   Yes, there is a significant problem.
2   There is some problem.
3   There is no problem at all.

The response to that type of question will very likely differ from the response to the preceding one, since it not only refers the question to professionals in general but also attempts to determine to what degree obsolescence may be a problem in an organization. In this regard it is interesting to note that more professionals were willing to indicate that they were not up to date than said that not keeping up with new developments constituted a significant problem among professionals.[7] Little bias is evident in such results, probably because of the anonymity of the questionnaire.

Rather than global attitude items, specific questions can be utilized to measure job assignment versus professional obsolescence. Examples of such questions, similar to those utilized by the author in studies of professional and job assignment obsolescence, are the following:

How up to date do you think you are with respect to knowledge and skills necessary to be effective in your *current work?*

1	2	3	4	5	6	7	8	9
Considerably less than is necessary		Slightly less than is necessary		About as much as is necessary		Slightly more than is necessary		Considerably more than is necessary

How up to date do you think you are with respect to knowledge and skills necessary for you to transfer effectively to a *new specialty* in your professional discipline?

1	2	3	4	5	6	7	8	9
Considerably less than is necessary		Slightly less than is necessary		About as much as is necessary		Slightly more than is necessary		Considerably more than is necessary

Although relatively good results have been obtained by using such items for measuring job assignment and professional obsolescence, even more specific measures can be created. It is possible to identify specific behaviors that are indicative of being obsolescent (or up to date) in a job or profession. The *critical incident* technique [8] is just one standard method that can be used to identify specific examples of obsolescent behavior. Attitude items based on those behaviors can be created and scored individually or combined to provide scores on a summated scale of obsolescence.

An attitude survey that includes any of the above types of measures, as well as questions pertaining to the organization, can also be used to identify organizational factors related to obsolescence. Therefore, attitude surveys are an excellent source of information for carrying out organizational analyses that not only measure obsolescence but also provide input to determine how the organization should respond to the problem.

Knowledge ratings. Attitude surveys, however, can provide only macro measures of obsolescence in the organization. In order to pinpoint specific deficiencies and strengths of individual professionals, either managerial or self-ratings of knowledge can be used. If the knowledge ratings are not anonymous, they can be used as an organization would use a skills inventory, namely, for measuring individual as well as organizational obsolescence. However, knowledge ratings provide an indication of a professional's *level* of competence in particular areas, whereas skills inventories usually indicate only whether the skill exists.

The following is an example of knowledge ratings that have been used to measure the degree to which professionals are aware of new or emerging fields.[9]

SUBJECT AREA	WHAT IS THE CURRENT STATE OF YOUR KNOWLEDGE IN THIS AREA?		
	EXTENSIVE	GENERAL	NONE
Information theory	1	2	3
Programmed learning	1	2	3
Critical path method	1	2	3
Matrices	1	2	3
Linear programming	1	2	3
Program evaluation and review techniques	1	2	3

Other questions that might be included in knowledge ratings of the preceding type could determine how effectively the knowledge is applied by the professional. It should be clear that, for organizations lacking skills inventories in their personnel records, knowledge ratings would provide similar but superior data. Such ratings can be tailor-made for professionals in a particular organization and can include subject areas necessary for measuring job assignment as well as professional obsolescence.

As will be discussed in later chapters, measures such as knowledge ratings can be utilized for individual placement and development. Figure 3 shows a personnel comparator in which ratings of the knowledge and skills of a candidate are compared with the requirements of a particular position. This

Figure 3   Personnel comparator.

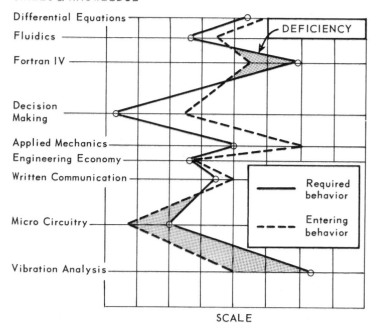

source: J. D. Boulgarides and V. C. San Filippo, "The Dilemma of Technical Obsolescence," Douglas Paper 4614M, Douglas Missile and Space Systems Division, October 1967, p. 13.

approach facilitates the identification of deficiencies and strengths relevant to a professional's effectiveness in a current or future position and thereby provides an adequate measure of obsolescence.

When they are obtained anonymously, knowledge ratings can describe the current level of knowledge and skills in the organization as a whole as well as in particular departments. The current level can be compared with future organizational needs for the purpose of forecasting the areas in which knowledge and skill deficiencies are likely to occur. This information can be invaluable for professional manpower planning and development as well as for bringing obsolescence under organizational control. Similar techniques can be applied to assessing individual and organizational training needs. (This is further elaborated in Chapter 7.)

Knowledge tests. Probably the most direct way to measure obsolescence is to use objective tests and assessment techniques that measure the degree to which an individual possesses the most up-to-date knowledge and skills necessary for his profession or job. However, since such tests are often difficult and expensive to develop, organizations might investigate the applicability of standardized paper-and-pencil tests, such as those used for professional licensing or for measuring competence in particular subject areas, and also tests of supervisory knowledge available from test publishers. It is likely, however, that such tests will be inappropriate for many, if not most, organizational professionals, particularly since they generally do not measure job assignment obsolescence.

The best approach for organizations that desire to measure obsolescence directly by means of knowledge tests would be to have the tests tailor-made, as other techniques of assessment would be. For example, methods of job analysis or critical incident techniques can be adapted for determining the knowledge and skills required by various professional job classifications in the organization, and that information can be utilized to develop tests of job assignment obsolescence.

Similarly, the knowledge and skills in particular areas not necessarily required at present but potentially useful in future job assignments can be obtained by probing and analyzing information collected from relevant individuals and published material. Such information can provide the basis for developing tests of professional obsolescence in each field.

A problem in using any of the preceding methods is that they too can become obsolete and must therefore be periodically updated. Because of the inherent difficulty and expense involved in their development, objective tests and assessments have rarely been used to measure obsolescence. One of the few attempts at creating an index of obsolescence in electrical engineering is briefly described by its developer:

> The first phase drew together, both nationally and internationally, that which has been done in this area, and it enabled us to build a criteria model. These criteria are the technologies that are regarded as current. . . . We validated the model with experts in the field, both in industry and at the university level. . . . We used this model with practicing electrical engineers who were selected because they are in a fast-growing field, and there are 32 specialties in this one area. With this model we constructed an index which could be used in making predictions.
>
> The concept of the obsolescence index (OI) is defined as the ratio between the current knowledge, as understood by the practitioner, and the current knowledge in the field. We may infer that when the OI equals 1, the practitioner is considered as being current. When the OI equals zero, the practitioner is considered as being obsolete.[10]

Another example of the development of an instrument that could be used for measuring obsolescence in personnel management focused on the latest knowledge of which personnel executives should be aware.[11] It consisted of statements containing information abstracted from current personnel management textbooks. The following are examples of items used in that measure of personnel management obsolescence:

Incentive plans generally result
in increased output and reduced costs. Agree ☐ Disagree ☐
Personality measures are better
predictors of job performance
than ability measures. Agree ☐ Disagree ☐
High job satisfaction is directly
related to high productivity. Agree ☐ Disagree ☐
Criticism by a superior is usu-
ally rejected as incorrect by
the employee. Agree ☐ Disagree ☐
The interview is the best method
of employee selection. Agree ☐ Disagree ☐

The interesting aspect of this type of test is that the statements appear to be opinions with which the personnel executives can either agree or disagree. An opinion format is certainly less threatening than something that looks like a test of
factual information. Also, it can more easily be included
as part of an attitude or opinion survey.

It is clear that the methods discussed thus far under organizational analyses can be part of a professional manpower survey that focuses on both attitudes and knowledge. Such a survey not only provides measures of obsolescence but also helps
to relate obsolescence to its causes and may even suggest
cures. That will become clearer in later chapters, where the
etiology of obsolescence is examined in greater depth.

Very likely the most developed of the test approaches to
measuring and dealing with obsolescence is the so-called job
knowledge survey.[12] The approach has been applied to supervisory as well as key nonmanagement-level jobs, and it appears highly appropriate as a measure of job assignment obsolescence in a wide variety of professional positions. The job
knowledge survey program follows an orderly plan that includes:

· Determining the job responsibility of a particular functional group.

- Outlining what knowledge is required to carry out that job responsibility.
- Developing a questionnaire to evaluate the depth of that job knowledge.
- Administering and analyzing the job knowledge questionnaires.
- Identifying job knowledge weaknesses on the basis of the questionnaire survey.
- Carrying out a training program based on job knowledge weaknesses revealed by individual performance on the questionnaire.

An example of an outline of the areas that should be covered in a job knowledge survey of packaging salesmen is shown in Figure 4. Several specific questions are then designed for each area in the outline, and they provide a clear picture of exactly what additional knowledge and skills packaging salesmen would need to carry out their job responsibilities more competently.

A sample list of questions developed for the job of manufacturing supervisor is given in Figure 5. It is rather clear from the sample questions that the job knowledge survey is tailor-made to deal specifically with job assignment obsolescence. Open-ended questions may be more difficult to score, but they allow professionals to demonstrate how much they really know about carrying out their job responsibilities.

The use of the job knowledge survey program has reportedly resulted in improved competence as exhibited by 16 percent or greater increase in productivity, 75 percent reduction in paperwork errors, and 60 percent decrease in customer complaints. It would appear that the technique could also be utilized to select and develop individuals for positions of increased responsibility. Therefore, the job knowledge survey could be integrated into the assessment center approach to evaluating and developing organizational professionals (see Chapter 4).

Although they are more costly, the various methods of or-

FIGURE 4   Sales job knowledge survey for packaging salesmen.

I. Packaging industry's market plan
II. Packaging salesman's responsibilities
III. Packaging industry information
   A. Packaging products
   B. Customers
   C. Customer services
   D. Pricing
   E. Competition
      1. Competitor's products
      2. Competitor's facilities
      3. Competitor's methods of packaging
      4. Competitive materials
IV. Company and product knowledge
   A. Company marketing organization
   B. Sales policies
      1. Closures and closure sheet
      2. Rigid containers
      3. Printed foil
      4. Flexible packaging
      5. Formed containers
   C. Manufacturing
      1. Facilities
      2. Equipment
      3. Products
      4. People
   D. R&D: facilities and organization
      1. ARL
      2. APDL
      3. AEDD
   4. Packaging design and engineering
   5. Packaging machinery
   6. Policies, procedures, functions
   7. Projects and priorities
   8. New-product development
   E. Marketing
      1. Marketing objectives
      2. Processes
         a. Food marketing
         b. Nonfood marketing
      3. Market services
         a. Graphics
         b. Commercial research
         c. Advertising, promotion, and trade relations
         d. New-product development
         e. New-product evaluation
V. Selling techniques
   A. Personal qualifications
   B. Managing time
   C. Choosing prospects
   D. The anatomy of a sale
   E. Buying situations
   F. Motivating sales
   G. Preparing for sales calls
   H. Finding the facts about a prospect's needs
   I. Skillful questioning and listening
   J. Creative selling

SOURCE: Terry Hartford, University of Pittsburgh.

FIGURE 5   Sample job knowledge survey questions, for manufacturing supervisor.

1. An employee refuses to perform an assigned duty that is within his classification. You are unable to persuade him to perform the work, and he threatens to leave the plant. What will you do:
   a. With respect to the employee?
   b. To get the work done?
2. At 7:00 P.M. a Maintenance foreman calls to advise that the No. 10 Mill lost 1,000 gallons of heavy lube oil. He says that he will need at least 800 gallons of replacement oil by 9:00 P.M. if the Mill is to stay in operation. You find only 200 gallons in stores. What will you do?
3. You receive a call from Maintenance stating that the reversing mill just went down due to a broken hydraulic component. The size of the replacement component requires the use of the stores mule train; however, you have no transportation available. What do you do?
4. Late on the midnight shift you find one of your most reliable employees asleep in Building 46. What action will you take?
5. A Maintenance foreman calls at 6 P.M. and advises you that "emergency" electrical components for the hot line are scheduled to arrive at 8:30 P.M. List the arrangements you will make for receiving.
6. Specify the type of seniority you would use to determine:
   a. Departmental transfer.
   b. Bidding within the department.
   c. Reduction of forces.
   d. Recall.
   e. Restoration of forces.
   f. Vesting for extended vacation.
7. A truckload of bags has arrived at the unloading dock. You observe that the bands have broken and the bags have slipped. What action will you take?
8. A truck is at the dock for unloading. Your safety committeeman complains that it is unsafe to unload. You investigate the alleged danger and it is your opinion that the truck can be unloaded safely. What do you do?

SOURCE: Terry Hartford, University of Pittsburgh.

ganizational analyses are certainly superior to personnel record data, especially since they provide direct measures of obsolescence and permit management to monitor and respond effectively to the problem. Furthermore, the cost of such analyses would be a mere fraction of the funds allocated for combatting obsolescence through a shotgun approach that relies on continuing education and training without an associated needs assessment. (See Chapter 7.)

OBSOLESCENCE HAS been defined as the degree to which organizational professionals lack the up-to-date knowledge or skills necessary to maintain effective performance in either current or future work roles. It is quite apparent from the discussion thus far that although obsolescence is a problem for many professionals in most organizations, it is a particularly acute problem for technical professionals and managers of specialized functions. However, indications are that it is becoming more serious among all professional groups. In the following chapters the specialists who have been most affected by obsolescence will be closely examined to see what lessons can be learned for professionals who are about to face the problem.

The question of measuring obsolescence has also been considered. We have seen that two general types of obsolescence indices have been used: (1) those that are based on information relatively accessible from personnel data systems and that are indirect measures at best and (2) more complicated techniques involving organizational analyses that provide direct measures of obsolescence. The most promising approaches appear to be those that utilize inventories, attitude surveys, ratings, or tests of knowledge and skills. Clearly, however, it would be more desirable to be able to prevent obsolescence rather than try to treat it after it has been detected. Prevention of obsolescence requires that its causes be known. That problem will be confronted in the next chapter, as well as in the chapters that follow it.

Chapter 3

Personal Characteristics, Obsolescence, and the Professional Career

PROFESSIONALS DIFFER not only in their degree of obsolescence but also in many other personal characteristics that may either predispose them to keep abreast with new developments or contribute to their going out of date. The participants in the First Conference on Occupational Obsolescence in 1966 recognized "that there is a need to isolate . . . some of the individual developmental factors that may or may not have influence on obsolescence," [1] but they had a wide variety of opinions about the specific factors involved.

Despite the passage of time since this plea was made, exploration of the extremely complex problem has not been widespread or sophisticated enough to have unequivocally isolated the most important personal characteristics facilitating or inhibiting obsolescence. Nevertheless, we can still discuss the factors that have been identified as possible individual causes of obsolescence. In this chapter the available empirical evidence will be examined for clues to the relationships between personal characteristics and obsolescence. Once those relationships are understood, management can utilize this knowledge by taking advantage of the individual differences among professionals to minimize obsolescence in the organization.

Age and Obsolescence: Reality or Myth?

Perhaps the most widespread assumption about obsolescence is that becoming out of date is an inevitable result of increasing age. The relationship between age and obsolescence is not a new subject; it was already a hot topic in management conferences almost half a century ago.[2] Acceptance of the assumption that obsolescence is inevitable with increasing age has institutionalized the viewpoint in company policies. A possible result is the self-fulfilling prophecy that, when professionals pass a certain age level, they are treated as irreversibly obsolescent and consequently behave that way without making any attempt at updating. An example of the assumption is this comment of a corporate executive: "I have given up on the 50- to 60-year-old management group, as far as combatting obsolescence is concerned. Now that technology in our industry has changed, there isn't sufficient time to help them."[3]

The attitudes toward age and obsolescence of nonsupervisory professionals are likely to be more extreme, as witness the following observation by an engineering manager: "If I had my way, I wouldn't have any engineers over 35 years old on my project. Engineering is a young man's game. Technology is changing so fast that our older engineers have fallen hopelessly behind."[4]

The implications of such attitudes are that once professionals reach middle age they are defined by management as obsolete and are assigned to the scrap heap. Although many individual cases can be cited to both support and refute that kind of thinking among management, there is conflicting empirical evidence that can generally be classified into one of three types of relationship between professional competence and age.

➤ 1. *Professional competence peaks early in the career.* Several studies have found that the best job performance and the maximum attainment in significant contributions and knowledge of new developments occur when the professionals are in their thirties and declines thereafter.[5] Some of the studies are widely known, and their conclusions are accepted by many managers. Other studies have found that older professionals are more likely to feel that their chief worry is keeping pace with new developments, that they are not fully qualified to handle their jobs, and that, when they lose their jobs, age becomes the most significant factor in determining how long they remain unemployed.[6] Such findings may reflect as well as reinforce the assumption that older professionals are more obsolescent.

2. *Professional competence peaks later in the career.* The second type of relationship found in several studies is a consistent upward trend in performance and professional output with increasing age that tends to reach a peak for those *over age 50.*[7] This is in clear contradiction to the decline in professional competence described in the preceding paragraph.

3. *Professional competence peaks both early and later in the career.* To further complicate matters, a third general finding is a relationship between age and performance that has been variously described as twin-peaked, saddle-shaped, or bimodal. Typically, what has been found is that performance is highest among professionals relatively early in their careers (that is, in their thirties), after which there is a drop-off in performance that is followed by a resurgence among those who are over age 50 and in the later stages of their professional life.[8]

The preceding results imply that there is not a simple clearcut relationship between increasing age and obsolescence. What may be relevant to the different relationships between professional competence and age is the so-called mid-life or mid-career crisis.[9] From the few research studies of mid-career development, it appears that the crisis period typically begins when professionals reach their thirties and is marked by feelings of personal frustration and failure. During this period many professionals perceive that what they have been doing is no longer fulfilling or important and that they have not attained the success in their careers that they expected. Such professionals feel they have little to look forward to in the future. It is during this period that careers, as well as marriages, go on the rocks and high rates of alcoholism, depression, suicide, and serious accidents occur. In fact, a peak in the death rate occurs between ages 35 and 40, and some have attributed it to the physical illness that is likely to accompany the emotional shock and severe depression that follow the individual's perception that he is on an irreversible downward path. Many professionals who experience the crisis, however, apparently continue to function usefully, and some even attain higher achievements later in their lives.

It has been suggested that the reason for a peak or a twin peak in performance early and later in careers may be that there are essentially two populations of professionals: one that declines rapidly with age and another that either maintains its performance or improves it over time. Among the first population are those who have not been able to cope with their mid-career crisis adequately, whereas those in the latter group either did not experience the crisis or resolved it successfully. When the two populations are pooled, the overall picture may be one of either deterioration or improvement with age, depending on how many of the professionals who experienced decline remain in the organizations studied. Some of those in the population that is declining may leave their organizations as well as their professions voluntarily or because of dismissals and forced retirements. If enough of those professionals drop out after they reach mid-career, the best performers tend to survive alone, which would explain the high average performance of older age groups in some studies. However, the survival of the fittest clearly does not occur in most organizations or professions, and consequently many of those who are obsolescent remain in their positions until they reach retirement age.

The speculation that there is a dual population, one that

stays abreast of current developments and another that becomes rapidly obsolescent, is supported by a study of professionals that reports that "while skills obsolescence was most in evidence among the middle and upper age groups, a sizable proportion of the 35 and over professionals have developed and do maintain currently required skills." [10] In fact, the evidence does show many older employees exceeding the performance of their younger colleagues.[11] Consequently, the assumption that obsolescence is an inevitable result of increasing age for all professionals is too simplistic and should be relegated to management mythology.

If in fact there are two populations, one that becomes obsolescent and another that stays up to date despite increasing age, it would be useful to know what factors contribute to the differential development. It may be most fruitful to examine the personal characteristics that have been associated with both obsolescence and age.

The Half-Life of a Professional Education

Related to increasing age is the half-life of a professional education, a concept borrowed from nuclear physics that has been widely used by writers to describe the extent to which obsolescence affects different professions. It has been defined as follows:

> The half-life of a professional's competence can be described as the time after completion of professional training when, because of new developments, practicing professionals have become roughly half as competent as they were upon graduation to meet the demands of their profession.[12]

In this view, then, it is the length of time that has elapsed since a professional has completed his education, rather than age, which is the crucial factor in his susceptibility to obsolescence. To illustrate this, a professional who has just completed his education at age 30 may very likely be more up to date than a 30-year-old colleague who has been out of school for almost ten years. Because the creation and application of new knowledge has been continually accelerating, the half-life of a professional education has been growing ever shorter. Studies of the changes in knowledge imparted by various professional disciplines have clearly demonstrated the phenomenon. As an example, the half-life of a chemical engineer's professional education in 1935 was almost 20 years, but by 1960 it had decreased to less than five years.[13] The rapid decrease of the half-life is depicted in Figure 6.

If this trend continues, some professional school graduates may already be obsolescent when they receive their degrees. Although that may sound absurd, it must be remembered that there is a time lag before new knowledge becomes integrated into professional curricula. All curricula undergo continual changes, and rapidly changing disciplines such as engineering and science have experienced discontinuous alterations in their educational content. It is the impact of the discontinuous change in the educational curriculum that tends to diminish the effectiveness of the older professional, as the following explanation indicates:

> The reason generally given for the fact that the skill deficiency problem is most serious among engineers and scientists over 35 is that these older professional technical people attended college prior to the middle 1950s and that it was only afterward that engineering colleges began to revise their curricula to give greatly increased emphasis to basic science and mathematics.[14]

This appraisal is corroborated by other researchers,[15] who have found not only that obsolescence among engineers is related to the number of years that have elapsed since they completed college, but also that the level of current knowledge tends to drop precipitously among those educated during and prior to the 1940s. Whereas the major alterations in technical curricula occurred in the 1950s, business and management education began to experience drastic revisions during the following decade. Increasing emphasis on quantitative and

FIGURE 6 The half-life of a chemical engineering education.

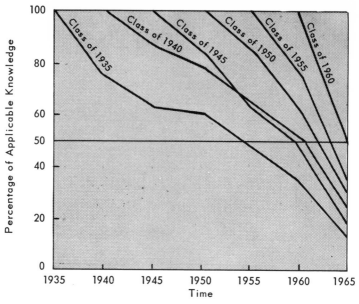

a: The amount of potential obsolescence as measured by the number of course additions and deletions in chemical engineering curricula.

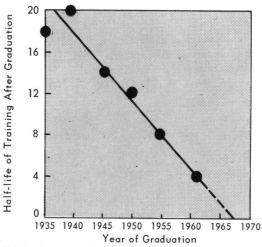

b: The half-life of a chemical engineer's training. (Data from *a.*)

operations research techniques, computer methodology, and behavioral science has likely reduced the half-life of a business and management education in much the same way that engineering was affected a decade earlier.

Although the half-life of a professional education may be the crucial factor in creating a susceptibility to obsolescence, there are clearly many professionals who have overcome the handicap of lack of knowledge in newly developed areas in their disciplines. To understand why that is so, it is necessary to delve more deeply into some of the personal characteristics that affect an individual's predisposition to obsolescence and are more psychological in nature.

Capacity for Knowledge Acquisition

An important psychological quality that facilitates or inhibits obsolescence among professionals is capacity for knowledge acquisition. The evidence is very clear that professional achievement and effectiveness are strongly related to an individual's knowledge acquisition potential as indicated by his intellectual and cognitive abilities.[16] Studies concerned with the diffusion of innovations have shown that the adoption of new ideas is more likely to occur among individuals who are more intelligent, have a greater ability to deal with abstractions, and possess more technical knowledge. Different types of abilities are very likely related to obsolescence, depending on the requirements of the particular professional occupation. For example, lack of proficiency in mathematics is associated with obsolescence among professionals in engineering and computer systems, whereas more general problem-solving abilities have been identified as important for management personnel.

Interviews with managers reveal that inadequate cognitive

SOURCE FOR FIGURE 6: S. S. Dubin, "The Psychology of Keeping Up-to-Date." Reprinted from *Chemtech*, July 1972, p. 394. Copyright by the American Chemical Society; reprinted by permission of the copyright owner.

ability is the most important personal characteristic that predisposes a professional to obsolescence. Moreover, a long-range study of career development has demonstrated that the cognitive strength that professionals bring to their first jobs will largely determine the degree to which they stay abreast of new knowledge during their subsequent careers. Indeed, some professionals may arrive at their first jobs in a state of actual or potential obsolescence as a result of their limited abilities in acquiring the requisite knowledge and skills. Such individuals will tend to choose work that does not require staying up to date and will thereby reinforce the likelihood of their becoming obsolescent. It has been found, for example, that engineers who have strong quantitative, verbal, and spatial abilities when they complete college end up in jobs that involve originating, developing, and testing ideas, whereas engineers who are poor in those abilities more often have jobs that put greater emphasis on estimating costs and controlling expenses. Professionals whose cognitive abilities are weak may be more obsolescence-prone to begin with, but the question that remains is what happens to those with superior abilities as they grow older.

It was long believed that various intellectual abilities decline among adults with advancing age, but that belief has recently been revised.[17] The inferior intellectual abilities frequently observed among older persons are very likely a result of their generally having had less education, since no such weakness appears among older but more educated groups. Indeed, there is evidence that professionals tend to exhibit an improvement in some intellectual abilities throughout their career, largely as a result of accumulated experience. Consequently, older professionals may in fact be superior to their younger colleagues, at least so far as cognitive strength is concerned.

However, some older professionals do become obsolescent despite the fact that their intellectual abilities may not have declined. Possessing a certain minimal level of appropriate cognitive abilities may be a necessary but not sufficient condition for remaining up to date, and consequently there must be other personal characteristics that can inhibit or enhance the acquisition of new knowledge by professionals. In the following section we will look at motivational and personality characteristics that are relevant to obsolescence.

Self-motivation to Stay Up to Date

The fact that some older professionals do have problems in keeping up to date with developments in their field, even when they have the ability to acquire new knowledge, may be attributed to an inadequate level of internal or self-motivation.[18] Motivation is the most widely discussed of all psychological characteristics associated with obsolescence, and the limited research evidence available tends to verify its importance and centrality. Interviews with managers representing a variety of technologically based organizations revealed that:

> . . . in addition to the lack of adequate educational grounding, other factors—personal or circumstantial—were deterring or preventing the skill-deficient professional technologists from updating their skills.
>
> In the view of many of the managers questioned on this point the failure to keep abreast of developments in the relevant field was due primarily to lack of motivation.[19]

Furthermore, among computer marketing and support personnel, who included both managers and nonsupervisory professionals, a lack of motivation was the most frequently cited factor in an individual's becoming out of date.

There is very clear evidence that those professionals who have a strong inner motivation do not experience the early decline often noted among those in their forties and tend to prolong their achievement over a broad span of their career. In fact, managers report that having that internal motivation is the most important personal characteristic associated with professionals who stay up to date. Ability factors were hardly mentioned for professionals who are up to date, which may indicate that although many may have the ability to keep abreast of new developments, it is primarily those with high motivation in that direction who actually do so. Lack of ability was cited most frequently as the characteristic of professionals who were obsolescent, but it is very likely that inadequate abilities are coupled with low motivation to develop or use those abilities. One may speculate that the cognitive deficiencies may be more visible and consequently are more often reported as a cause of obsolescence.

Moreover, professionals may be motivated in different directions, some of which may lead more readily to obsolescence. Indeed, psychologists have utilized various concepts to explain why individuals behave in different ways, and an analysis of some of these motivational factors is crucial to understanding the causes of obsolescence. Aspects of motivation that affect obsolescence include differences among professionals with respect to interests, needs, goals, energy, and initiative.

INTEREST DIFFERENCES

By the time professionals begin their college education, they develop patterns of interest that remain highly stable throughout most of their careers.[20] These patterns of interest not only help determine occupational choice but also influence the professional's job function, level of responsibility, performance, and innovativeness. For example, engineers with strong interests in people and economics rather than in things or ideas tend to become employed in jobs that emphasize the development and utilization of personnel or the estimation of costs and the control of expenses, whereas engineers who have strong interests in abstract ideas but not in people tend to become involved in work in which they originate, develop, and test ideas.

Among managers, those who are more effective have interests in activities that involve independent and intense thinking, risk-taking, and social relationships in which they are dominant, but they dislike activities requiring regimentation and the performance of technical or detailed tasks. The opposite types of interest patterns among engineers working in development, as compared with those in sales, determine the effectiveness or lack of effectiveness in each function. More specifically relevant to obsolescence is the fact that interest patterns are associated with the degree to which professionals set the development of new ideas as their most important goal, as well as with their preference for reading professional books for pleasure as opposed to other books. Moreover, interest tends to influence the pursuit of continuing professional education.

It is rather clear that the degree to which professionals engage in activities likely to keep them up to date with new developments is influenced by their fundamental interests, which develop and stabilize well before they launch their careers. Recruiters should be aware of this when they are hiring new graduates. The use of such information in selection and placement will be discussed in the next chapter. Although there is strong evidence that cognitive factors may be more crucial than interest patterns in determining whether professionals keep current with new knowledge, both factors may become important during the mid-career period. Professionals who have the ability as well as the interest to acquire new knowledge may be able to pass through the mid-career period unscathed and go on to attain high levels of professional competence and achievement. Nonetheless, interests represent a rather global orientation toward one's career, and it may be more instructive to turn to the more fundamental aspects of motivation that are more sensitive to change and consequently more relevant to obsolescence.

CHANGES IN NEEDS

Whereas interests and abilities tend to remain relatively stable during a professional's career, that does not appear to be true of needs that the professional strives to satisfy.[21] Different needs have been identified as motivators of behavior, and certainly in management theory the most widely known of such needs are those that have been identified by Maslow,

McGregor, and Herzberg. In their simplest terms needs can be classified as either lower-level security needs or higher-order growth needs, and the strengths of both kinds have been found to change during the professional's career. For example, the more basic lower-order protective needs that involve the need to feel safe, secure, and avoid threat tend to be relatively strong at the very beginning of the professional career but then sharply diminish in strength within five years. However, during that period the higher-order needs for growth that include the attaining of achievement, esteem, and self-development increase significantly in intensity regardless of career success.

At the beginning of his career, the professional may have a strong need to establish himself securely in his organization, in which he initially experiences anxiety, uncertainty, and stress. However, it generally does not take him very long to adapt to his organizational role and become integrated into the new environment. Consequently, the need for security diminishes in intensity as this early stage in his career passes and he begins to feel comfortable in the organization. Thereafter, his needs for attaining esteem and achievement begin to increase, so that quite early in his career these growth needs become the most intense. It is likely that the stronger his growth needs, the weaker his predisposition toward becoming obsolescent. This is implied by the fact that individuals with high achievement needs are more dependent on their own skill for success, are more willing to take risks, assume greater individual responsibility for making decisions, and tend to anticipate future exigencies by taking current action with respect to those future developments. Therefore, it is not surprising that such individuals tend to become successful in business organizations, in addition to staying up to date and attaining high levels of competence in their fields.

However, not all professionals are able to satisfy their growth needs. By the fifth year, those whose careers are successful are able to satisfy their growth needs, whereas the satisfaction of such needs plummets among those who do not experience career success. That could very well be the initial stage of the mid-career crisis experienced by some professionals upon reaching their thirties. If the frustration of growth needs continues into the mid-career stage, the higher-order needs may be replaced by the protective security needs—a defensive response to the anxiety caused by lack of career success.

The return to an earlier stage of career development among chronically unsuccessful professionals is a process akin to psychological regression. The individual who has regressed seeks to protect or restore his self-confidence by satisfying needs that have been successfully dealt with in the past. It is noteworthy that unsuccessful, as compared with successful, professionals have significantly stronger security needs at the beginning of their careers, which possibly indicates that their lack of success may be influenced at an early stage by a need to avoid failure. They may continue to concentrate on satisfying security needs and thereby neglect their growth needs.

A reduction in growth needs may also eventually occur among professionals who have successfully satisfied those needs, and other types of needs may emerge as important later in the career. The professional who has attained career success may then strive to direct his efforts to some higher-order cause that may involve service to his profession, organization, family, community, or society. As the growth needs level off and reach a plateau, another critical period in the professional's career emerges, and the direction it takes will greatly influence the degree to which obsolescence will occur.

There are important differences as well as shifts in the way needs may be satisfied at different career stages. Therefore, it would be more fruitful at this point to expand the discussion of needs to include an examination of the changing nature of career goals as a response to changing needs.

CHANGES IN CAREER GOALS

Individuals attempt to satisfy their needs by seeking certain goals.[22] Workers who are college-educated, as compared with those who are not, have goals that are more oriented to doing challenging work, developing their abilities, and attaining professional growth. There are also career-goal differences among the various professions. A difference in goal orientation already exists at the very beginning of the person's career, largely as a consequence of the nature of the chosen profession and of the different socialization and educational processes that occur during and prior to attending college. For example, being able to continue education at the graduate level appears to be a more important goal for new engineering graduates than for graduates in accounting, although the latter clearly go through a continuing education process in attaining their CPA certification, and do desire in-house training programs. However, the most important goals for new college graduates, regardless of degree major, are opportunities to engage in the type of work that will provide both challenges and opportunities for advancement. Those goals are subject to change during the career depending on whether they are achieved. Individual goals are also influenced by the goal emphasis in the organization, and there is a socialization process whereby the individual's goals become more congruent with those of the organization.

To simplify this discussion, goals that can satisfy growth needs may be classified as either (1) oriented to the individual's organization or (2) directed to his profession. In the terms most commonly used by sociologists, those goals are either "local" or "cosmopolitan" in nature. Goals associated with an organizational or local career orientation include doing work that involves contributions to company success, learning about the organization's methods and procedures, and attaining organizational influence through advancement.

Professional or cosmopolitan goals include doing work that involves exploring new ideas, using and learning new knowledge, and establishing a reputation outside the company as an authority in one's field. Although a few organizational professionals can be classified as having either pure local or pure cosmopolitan goals, most have a mixture of both. The emphasis in goal orientation, however, is dependent to some degree on professional group membership. Managers and business professionals tend to have a commitment toward organizational goals, although that does not preclude cosmopolitan goals, particularly among those who are specialists. By comparison, technical professionals tend to have a more cosmopolitan goal orientation than business professionals. However, goals differ among technical professionals. Engineers are more strongly committed to organizational goals, and scientists tend to have goals more in line with those of their professional colleagues. Regardless of an individual's specialty, however, a cosmopolitan orientation tends to increase strongly among those with advanced education in their fields, and it reaches its peak among those at the doctoral level.

It should be emphasized that cosmopolitan and local goals do not necessarily have to conflict. When organizational goals and the goals of the professional coincide, as they do in many specialties, success in the organization often accompanies success in the specialty. Even to cosmopolitan-oriented scientists, promotion in the organization is often of equal importance with professional success. Professional orientation and organizational success do go hand in hand, judging by studies which show that demoted managers stand out by their lack of professional identification. Indeed, growth needs can be satisfied by attaining goals that are local, cosmopolitan, or both, depending on the individual's orientation. However, obsolescence, especially of the professional type, is most likely to occur among those who lack some degree of cosmopolitan goal orientation with its focus on doing work involving new ideas, acquiring new knowledge, and attaining professional recognition.

As the career progresses, goals tend to change, and there is increasing emphasis on organizational commitment as well as an accommodation between organizational and professional goals. The process of change in goals with increasing age is evident from a study of engineers who exhibit both local and cosmopolitan orientation, but with a varying emphasis at different stages of their career. The desire to work on projects requiring new technical learning is the most important goal of younger engineers but rapidly diminishes in importance as a goal among older age groups, so that it is no longer important after mid-career. On the other hand, helping the company to increase its profits is ranked as the most important goal only among those who have passed their mid-career stage, a group which puts employment stability among its most important goals. The decreasing desire to work on projects requiring new learning and the increased orientation toward company goals and security appear to be both causes and effects of obsolescence. As we shall see, however, the organization plays a major role in shaping such changes.

Studies of other professionals have demonstrated that goals related to satisfying growth needs, such as promotion or getting a different job, diminish in importance throughout the career. Growth-oriented goals cease to be important for those over age 50, for whom stability and retirement goals become important. Such changes of major goals during the career are likely to be accompanied by considerable stress, beginning with the organizational shock the newly hired professional experiences when he realizes that his work is incompatible with his career expectations. Although the satisfaction of growth needs may initially be oriented toward work goals having to do with acquiring new knowledge, many professionals do not attain those goals. Often that is because their work does not require them to, as will be discussed in Chapter 5. By mid-career, professionals who have not kept up to date may look for other means of satisfying their growth needs, very likely by seeking local goals such as advancement. When professionals reach a stage in their careers when neither cosmopolitan nor local goals are attainable, they will seek goals which assure their employment security and stability. By that point, they may be in such an advanced state of obsolescence that attempts at updating might be fruitless.

In fact, professionals who do not achieve their important goals feel it is because their training is becoming out of date.

The obsolescence that begins to increase sharply during mid-career may actually be a syndrome that involves a number of factors associated with lack of goal attainment. Professionals who feel that their goals are not being achieved because their training is becoming out of date also are likely to feel that they may not have the abilities required to achieve their goals, that their opportunities to advance have become more limited, and that management has classified them as not being able to handle broader responsibility. The net results of such feelings of anxiety about lack of goal attainment are the motivational and ultimately the personality changes that occur among some older professionals. One such change affects the amount of energy the professional is willing to invest in goal attainment.

CHANGES IN ENERGY AND INITIATIVE

A lack or loss of energy has been identified as another factor that predisposes professionals to obsolescence.[23] Motivation implies that energy must be expended to attain the goals that will in turn gratify individual needs. The more difficult the goals, the greater the energy that must be directed toward their attainment. Several research studies have found that professional success is associated with the amount of energy expended at work, which is usually evidenced by a professional's willingness to work hard for long hours. Psychologists have concluded not only that the more successful professionals have a considerable amount of energy available, but also that this energy is channeled into intellectual forms of satisfaction. Energy is expended as long as goals are perceived as attainable. The evidence seems to be clear that many older individuals not only have less energy to invest than those who are younger but also have less reason to invest energy in the attainment of goals because, by middle age, many career goals either have been attained or have become too difficult to reach. The expenditure of a diminishing amount of energy to keep from becoming obsolete may not even be relevant to the goals of many older professionals, who, as we have seen, can become more interested in their own security and less growth-oriented.

Some investigators have suggested that a professional's initiative is tied in with energy level, and is an important personal characteristic that contributes to the expenditure of energy in updating activities.[24] Initiative involves not only the beginning of actions but also the capacity to note and discover new means of goal attainment. The professional with a high degree of initiative is able to act independently and undertake actions to attain goals without support and stimulation from others. The professional also has the capacity to see new courses of action as well as ways of implementation which are not readily apparent to others. The self-generating aspects of initiative contribute not only to professional success but to independent efforts in updating activities as well. Although initiative does tend to diminish among older professionals, the evidence shows that for some individuals, initiative may even increase with age. Organizational success and professional goal attainment appear to reinforce initiative well into the later career stages.

The degree to which individuals attain their major goals affects their adjustment to the environment. In essence this adjustment involves the various aspects of personality that help determine, and, in turn, are affected by the way the individuals go about attaining their goals. It is in the area of personality that this examination of the individual factors contributing to obsolescence will be completed.

Personality and Obsolescence

Personality factors have been identified as the major cause of failure among executives.[25] However, it is in the area of personality that the greatest paucity of hard data exists, and this discussion must of necessity be more speculative. Although few if any researchers have focused specifically on personality characteristics and obsolescence, it appears that among the most important of such factors are (1) the individual's self-concept and (2) the way in which he responds to change and uncertainty.

SELF-CONCEPT

As individuals learn that they can effectively master the challenges of their environment, feelings of competence, self-esteem, and confidence emerge as integral parts of their self-concepts.[26] That in turn will lead to their pursuing more difficult and more challenging goals. Conversely, the opposite type of self-concept may emerge among those who do not effectively act upon their environments to attain their goals. The need for attaining a positive self-concept results in individuals seeking goals that will enhance their competence and self-esteem, and avoiding the pursuit of goals that are likely to diminish their self-concept. An individual's self-concept is an important determinant not only of his occupational choice but also of his attainment of competence and career success.

The professional's self-concept will also influence his behavior toward keeping abreast of new developments. Those with high self-esteem will tend to be more concerned with maintaining competence in their fields and seek out the more challenging goals concerned with professional development to satisfy their own growth needs. Professionals who have low self-esteem may be more concerned with protecting their feelings of competence and may therefore seek goals that will help them avoid failure. Such goals satisfy security needs rather than growth needs.

Professionals who begin their careers with high self-assurance are significantly more satisfied with their attainment of professional aspirations and recognition, as well as management aspirations later in their career, than are those who have low self-assurance. Consequently, individuals have a predisposition toward increasing their competence prior to their first work experience, and this may play an important role in determining whether or not they become obsolescent. Professionals who start out with high self-esteem will very likely become more competent and up to date than those whose self-esteem is low. By successfully attaining competence in new areas, the professional with high self-esteem will feel sufficiently confident to seek opportunities to become competent in additional new areas. On the other hand, the professional with low self-esteem will want to do work with which he is familiar and in which he feels confident, but he will tend to avoid acquiring new and unfamiliar knowledge and skills that may reveal how much he does not know. This becomes a vicious cycle, since by avoiding updating activities the professional becomes more obsolescent and more insecure and more anxious to protect his position and self-image.

Although a loss of self-confidence can be an important factor in obsolescence, there is no clear-cut indication that self-confidence diminishes with age. Indeed, older people are often more self-confident than younger ones. What is clear is that a high degree of self-confidence helps the professional resist the erosion that may accompany advancing age.

STYLES OF RESPONDING TO CHANGE

The increasing proliferation of information, coupled with continuous organizational restructuring, creates a climate that requires the professional to be able to cope with new developments, change, and the inevitable uncertainty which is a concomitant of change. There is some evidence that certain personality attributes are related to the degree to which the individual can successfully adjust to change and uncertainty. One such attribute is the willingness to take risks or its converse, cautiousness.[27] The fear of taking any risk has, in fact, been identified by managers as an important contributing cause of obsolescence. One researcher who has explored why individuals are open to new ideas and innovations reports that

> . . . venturesomeness is almost an obsession with innovators. They are eager to try new ideas. . . . The major value of the innovator is venturesomeness. He must desire the hazardous, the rash, the daring, and the risking. The innovator must also

be willing to accept any occasional debacle when one of the new ideas he adopts proves unsuccessful.[28]

The professional who actively keeps abreast of new developments and copes successfully with change should have at least a moderate propensity for risk taking in addition to not fearing failure. Studies have demonstrated that organizational output is detrimentally affected by low-risk-taking behavior, and that employees who are high risk takers have a greater tolerance for change, perform better under changing conditions, and are more inclined to seek and accept jobs that are different from their prior experience than those who avoid taking risks. The willingness of organizational professionals to take risks is also associated with a strong need for achievement and a low fear of failure, characteristics that have already been linked with the professional's motivation to stay up to date.

As is true of the individual's self-concept, it is very likely that the risk-taking propensity has already evolved as a fundamental part of personality prior to the beginning of the professional career. Nevertheless, there is some evidence that cautiousness tends to increase among older professionals. In a study of managers from 200 corporations, it was found that the youngest were most willing to take risks and the oldest were least willing. The greatest decline in managerial risk taking occurs between the early twenties and the early thirties. Thereafter, willingness to take risks remains rather stable, although a sharp decrease occurs again among managers who are beyond their late forties. Beyond that age, cautiousness can become very debilitating to a professional's contributions.

It may be surmised that younger professionals have fewer responsibilities and the most to gain by taking risks. They are also less likely to be afraid to venture into new and unfamiliar aspects of their fields, and they therefore tend to remain abreast of new developments. The increased cautiousness exhibited by those in mid-career may be associated with the feeling that there is little to gain and a great deal to lose if they take high risks and fail. Consequently, they tend to use methods and techniques with which they are already familiar, and they thereby limit their exposure to new knowledge and skills. This behavior may reach its extreme among some of those over 50 since, on the average, older professionals tend to exhibit the greatest cautiousness. It should be emphasized, however, that there is a great deal of variability in risk taking at each age level. Consequently, there are some older professionals who maintain their willingness to take risks and are less cautious than individuals among the younger groups.

Rigidity is another important characteristic associated with obsolescence, since it can impair the professional's ability to cope with change.[29] Even worse, rigidity or lack of flexibility in the face of change may lead to resisting change and attempting to carry out work tasks according to past practices rather than new requirements. Professionals who become obsolescent include not only those who are unable to change because of inadequate training but also those who are unwilling to change despite their ability to do so. In fact, executives have identified reluctance to change as one of the important factors contributing to obsolescence.

Openness to new ideas, originality, and creativity are associated with greater flexibility and, conversely, with lower rigidity. Moreover, a lack of flexibility or adaptability has been associated with ineffectiveness of various types of professionals. Rigidity has been found to increase with age, particularly in the early forties age group and again in groups over fifty, but as in the case of risk taking, some older individuals may be more flexible than their younger colleagues. Adjustment to change, coping with new environments, and career success have also been found to be associated with an individual's tolerance for ambiguity or uncertainty.[30] That trait fits into a consistent personality portrait of the obsolescent professional, namely, one involving a defensive response style to change. Professionals who do not want to take risks, have a rigid, inflexible approach to the world around them, and have difficulty in dealing with uncertainty will almost certainly perceive change as a potential threat. These professionals will tend to seek out a stable, unchanging environment in which they feel safe but where their growth will stagnate.

ONE FACT which has thus far emerged rather clearly is that there are important personal characteristics which predispose professionals to become obsolescent. It would appear that some professionals already have "built-in obsolescence" characteristics before they even begin their careers. Those characteristics have been identified in this chapter as follows:

- A limited capacity for knowledge acquisition that is determined by the individual's intellectual and cognitive abilities.
- A lack or loss of internal motivation to stay up to date that is related to the individual's interests, needs, goals, energy, and initiative.
- Personality predispositions that involve a weak self-concept and poor adaptability to change.

Although some personal characteristics, such as intellectual abilities and general interests, remain relatively stable during a professional's career, the important motivational and personality characteristics tend to change as the career progresses. However, as we have seen, obsolescence does not necessarily have to accompany increasing age. Awareness of the personal characteristics relevant to obsolescence and their changes during a professional's career may help management to understand the individual causes of obsolescence and such related phenomena as the mid-career crisis. However, it is natural to ask the question of how organizations can best utilize that knowledge in their day-to-day operations. What, for example, are the implications of the fact that some professionals are obsolescence-prone · to begin with? Some suggestions that pertain to these questions are offered in the next chapter, which focuses on personnel management practices for controlling obsolescence.

Chapter 4

Personnel Practices for Controlling Obsolescence

In the preceding chapter, an attempt was made to identify and examine the most important personal characteristics which contribute to the obsolescence of a professional's knowledge and skills. Although this information may be useful for the individual manager in detecting obsolescence-prone subordinates, it may also be utilized by organizations as an informational input to their operational practices. As will be demonstrated, differences in personal characteristics need not be a major problem for the organization. Instead, they can be capitalized upon to allow for more effective goal attainment by both the organization and its professionals.

A number of personnel management methods can be adapted to deal with the personal characteristics associated with obsolescence. This chapter will focus on some current management practices that can utilize differences in personal characteristics for bringing obsolescence under organizational control. In particular, we will look at techniques of selection and placement, assessment, career counseling, and retirement practices.

Selection and Placement to Reduce Obsolescence

One of the best ways in which an organization can capitalize on individual differences to minimize obsolescence is to institute effective techniques of selection and placement.[1] In fact, when executives were asked how obsolescence could be eliminated or alleviated in their organizations, there was strong support for the selection and placement approach, as illustrated by the following responses:

> We should select men who have capabilities for development, and these men should be the ones placed in responsible positions. In my judgment, it is the responsibility of the company to recognize at an early date the man's deficiency and take action before he becomes a fixture in some one location.[2]
>
> .　　.　　.
>
> The only preventative is better selection for the position. . . . If there is any doubt about the ability or potential of the individual using as many aids in judgment as possible, he should not be chosen. . . . By aids in judgment, I refer to personality tests, intelligence tests, nondirective interviews, work performance as judged by several management people.[3]

Placing newly hired professionals in positions for which they lack the appropriate ability, motivation, and personality practically guarantees the emergence of obsolescence not too long after they begin their organizational careers.

The selection process constitutes an input control on the quality of an organization's professional manpower. Too often, manpower quality control has been exercised superficially; it has focused primarily on meeting immediate organizational needs rather than longer-range requirements. Perhaps the most compelling reason not to utilize more stringent selection procedures has been the shortage of qualified candidates, particularly among technical professionals. New graduates were courted by organizations, many of which were merely trying to fill a head count, and the only qualification necessary was a degree in a particular field.

That situation has changed drastically, beginning with the

widespread scarcity of positions in many professional fields during the early 1970s. Since there was a surplus of certain professionals in the labor market, organizations were in a position to be highly selective in filling their available positions with the most appropriate applicants. But even under the most optimal labor market circumstances, some organizations have avoided the use of selection techniques that can help limit long-range organizational obsolescence.

Resistance by professionals to such selection techniques as tests and reluctance by management to invest in validating selection and placement programs that appear to be rather complex and costly are just two of the possible reasons why organizations have not used such techniques. Yet selection decisions based on some type of information about job candidates are nevertheless still made. The cost of developing more effective methods for making such decisions must be weighed against the later costs of obsolescence that result from professionals being mismatched in their jobs. Moreover, if organizations are concerned about resistance to testing, they can utilize certain nontest techniques which are widely employed to collect information on applicants.

In a pool of candidates for professional-level positions there is usually a distribution of individuals who possess a range of abilities, motivations, and personality predispositions. Similarly, the positions in an organization vary in the individual qualities they require of their incumbents to fulfill present and future job demands successfully. Some jobs have continually changing demands, whereas others are relatively stable. Professionals who are more flexible and inclined toward risk taking should be placed in the changing environment, whereas those who are more rigid and cautious are more appropriate for the relatively stable positions. Furthermore, many professional jobs do not require the application of the latest knowledge and skills. Professionals whose abilities, interests, goals, and other qualities indicate high promise for succeeding in positions that require keeping up to date should be selected for those types of positions. To attain such a matching, organizations can apply various techniques of personnel selection and placement oriented to future manpower development.

Perhaps the most appropriate step to start with would be a job analysis of professional positions but with a focus on future job requirements, particularly for those functions that are likely to undergo the greatest change. The personal attributes that would be required for professionals to change successfully with those positions would have to be identified. A considerable amount of judgment and insight is necessary to forecast the future nature of job requirements. Job forecasting, like technological forecasting, may well be worth the effort, since both can help prevent organizational obsolescence through long-range planning for future manpower skill requirements.

Once the future requirements of jobs are determined and the personal attributes necessary for successful performance of those jobs are identified, selection decisions characteristically are attempts to make predictions about an applicant's future behavior based on evidence of past or present behavior. Many standard selection methods are available. Their roles in diminishing obsolescence will be briefly discussed below.

THE APPLICATION BLANK

The application blank is among the most widely used sources of information about an applicant's past experiences. The responses to items on the blank can be scored to predict the likelihood of obsolescence in particular jobs or functions. The so-called weighted application blank that uses scored items has long been utilized as an input to the making of selection decisions. Since application blanks are generally kept on file for professionals hired during some preceding period, the responses to the items can be related to some relevant measure of current obsolescence among individuals in a particular functional area. Some of the measures discussed in Chapter 2, such as the skills inventory and knowledge tests, could be utilized as criteria or indices of obsolescence. By properly applying appropriate statistical techniques, it is possible to produce an application blank that can contribute to the prediction of professional competence in different functional specialties.

THE BIOGRAPHICAL INVENTORY

The biographical inventory is an extension of the weighted application blank, but it typically collects more detailed information about prior experiences and may include current attitudes and interests. As in the case of the application blank, a biographical inventory may be constructed, generally by utilizing a multiple-choice format, to predict obsolescence in particular specialties. The weighting of the items that discriminate between the professionals who are likely to stay up to date and those who are not is similar to that used with the application blank.

Biographical inventories have been highly successful in predicting competence among different professionals. The fact that they permit the measurement of various motivational and personality characteristics, including interests, needs, energy level, self-concept, and reactions to challenging or unstructured work situations, makes them ideal instruments for identifying many of the individual differences that contribute to obsolescence. Since changes are always occurring in both the nature of jobs and the composition of the labor market, the weighting of both application blanks and biographical inventories should be reviewed periodically to account for such changes.

THE EMPLOYMENT INTERVIEW

The employment interview is universally accepted as a technique that contributes to the selection decision. However, because of its questionable validity in the making of selection decisions, its role in controlling obsolescence in the organization may be limited. Nevertheless, the interview can be used to elicit information relevant to career potential and fill in gaps that cannot be easily obtained by other techniques. For example, the interviewer can probe in depth the applicant's immediate and long-range career goals. By comparing these with the opportunities in the organization, he can decide whether the two are compatible. Questions that focus on professional knowledge can be presented systematically and evaluated to determine the competence of the applicant.

Moreover, the interview is a two-way exchange of information. Not only should the applicant be encouraged to communicate relevant background information, but the interviewer should accurately describe what the organization expects of its professionals, and also the prospects for future career development. An applicant may realize that the expectations of the organization will be in conflict with his career goals. Under those circumstances it is better for all concerned that he reject the prospect of working under conditions that are likely to frustrate his goal attainment. The effectiveness of the interview can be improved by careful selection and training of interviewers, in addition to the use of patterned, structured interviews. If the interview is properly utilized, it may provide information about future potential that is not available from other sources.

REFERENCES AND BACKGROUND CHECKS

References and background checks are sometimes-useful sources of information that are routinely used in selection decisions. Unfortunately, there has been difficulty in the use of references as a selection technique, primarily because references tend to provide very positive evaluations of candidates. However, there are a number of ways in which the use of references can be improved to predict future potential. Professional references, such as former supervisors or teachers, generally provide more valid and critical information about the potential capabilities of prospective employees than do personal references. When a reference provides positive statements about such traits as an individual's dependability, vigor, and ability, they usually indicate that he has a potential for successful performance. If only characteristics such as cooperation and consideration are mentioned, there may be some question about the future success of the candidate.

Investigations of candidates made in person or by telephone generally yield more complete and accurate information than written recommendations. For example, a professional's lack of competence would probably never be mentioned in a written communication but would almost certainly be mentioned in a personal interview. Although interviews with former superiors or teachers who have had the opportunity to observe the qualities of the candidate can be costly, they may turn out to be one of the most revealing sources of information regarding a professional's future potential and career success.

PSYCHOLOGICAL TESTING

Psychological testing can provide objective measures of the various attributes that may predispose a professional to obsolescence. Tests of cognitive abilities can be effective in identifying the candidates who stand a good chance of being successful in the most intellectually demanding positions. Since professionals are generally a select group with high intelligence to begin with, only the most difficult tests of cognitive abilities will be able to effectively discriminate the most competent from the rest. In this regard, achievement or competence tests that measure proficiency in the application of knowledge in a particular field are especially useful. Tests of knowledge in such diverse specialties as mathematics, engineering, and accounting exist, and others may be tailor-made as part of a professional selection test battery. Tests of ability and competence can assure that the organization is hiring professionals who possess the intellectual strength and knowledge that are necessary to stay up to date with new developments. Such tests generally can have dual roles by providing information for selection decisions as well as helping to determine the placement of accepted applicants in appropriate jobs.

Various standardized tests and measurements of interests and personality are more relevant for placement or as counseling tools than for providing information for the selection decision. If candidates are administered interest inventories or personality tests after they are hired and are made to realize that the results will be used for their development and counseling, then there will be a greater likelihood of eliciting honest responses. Such tests may identify the qualities that will help determine whether a professional will be motivated to stay up to date in a particular specialty and therefore assist in guiding and placing him in the most appropriate position. The establishment of a testing program to reduce obsolescence may require the services of a competent psychologist plus supporting personnel. The costs involved in testing, or in other selection techniques, should be weighed against the benefits in reducing obsolescence. Even if tests are utilized, they are merely one input, albeit an important one, to the complex decision process involved in the effective initial selection and placement of professionals designed to control obsolescence.

Assessment and Career Counseling

After professionals are hired and placed in permanent positions, there are various techniques of assessment and career counseling which can be used for individual development and improvement.[4] By monitoring the progress of professionals and by helping the individual make correct career decisions, organizations can more easily keep obsolescence in check. In fact, executives identify employee appraisals and development as the two best methods for alleviating obsolescence.

Practically all organizations use some type of performance appraisal, and many of the appraisals are highly formalized. They are used for making important manpower decisions concerning merit increases, promotions, transfers, training and development, demotions, terminations, and retirements. The traditional methods of performance appraisal have been widely criticized, and they appear to be of limited use in combatting obsolescence. Performance appraisals generally require the supervisor to play the role of judge, which often interferes with and damages the counseling or coaching relationship between the professional and his manager, which is an increasingly important part of the manager's role. Since performance appraisals are typically used for promotion, discharge, and salary decisions as well as for developing and improving individuals, the superior is required to play roles of both judge and counselor, which are incompatible and consequently become ineffective. In fact, there is evidence that when a superior in this dual role provides critical feedback in the performance review, the result tends to be poorer rather than improved performance among subordinates.

To avoid some of the pitfalls of the traditional performance appraisal approach, organizations can attempt to separate the judge and counseling roles. The separation may be accomplished by applying some of the more recently developed techniques such as (1) assessment centers, which are responsible for appraisals but diminish the manager's role as judge, and (2) the management-by-objectives approach, which emphasizes the counseling and coaching relationship between superior and subordinate.

ASSESSMENT CENTERS

Unlike most appraisal techniques, assessment centers evaluate future career potential rather than past performance; consequently, they are highly appropriate means by which obsolescence can be detected and prevented in the organization.[5] The application of assessment center methodology goes back to the Office of Strategic Services in World War II and the pioneering work by AT&T in industry beginning in the mid-1950s, but it was not until the decade of the 1970s that assessment centers began to be accepted for use in managerial appraisal in organizations of all types. That they have been so widely accepted is very likely the result of the undisputed evidence that their accuracy in choosing employees for promotions and transfers to positions of greater responsibility is clearly superior to that of other methods. Typically, assessment centers bring together nonsupervisory personnel or lower-level managers for a period of several days, during which the employees participate in situational exercises relevant to performance in higher-level managerial positions. Meanwhile, they are being observed and rated by trained appraisers. In addition, the centers may administer psychological tests and conduct interviews to make a more complete assessment of each candidate's future potential.

Not only have assessment centers been highly accurate in predicting future success, but they have tended to equalize opportunities for candidates to demonstrate their strengths under fair conditions. Reducing bias in judging candidates, which often exists when the superior makes the appraisal, reportedly has had positive effects on morale and job expectations. Bias in choosing candidates for the assessment itself can be reduced by using self-nominations rather than managerial selection, a technique which has been quite successful in several organizations.

The use of assessment centers is likely to increase rapidly. It is spurred on by the necessity of complying with the Equal Employment Opportunity Commission requirements that there must be a demonstrable relationship between placement and promotion methods and later job performance. There is also potential cost saving to the organization. The costs of assessment centers are declining with the increasing availability of packaged assessment programs, some of which require an investment of less than $300 per candidate. An example of such a package is the Assessment Center Program for Evaluating Supervisory Potential distributed by the American Management Associations.

Although there is no existing program that focuses specifically on career development to avoid obsolescence, it would appear to be a relatively easy matter to include the measurement of professional knowledge and skills as well as adaptability to change in an assessment center program. Assessment centers currently focus on leadership skills, which are generally more difficult to measure than professional knowledge and skills. Typically, professionals are assumed to be competent in the knowledge and skills relevant to their specialties or jobs before they are selected to participate in the center, and hence these characteristics are not even measured. This is a needless omission, since professional knowledge and skills, as well as job knowledge and skills, can be measured by objective techniques such as the knowledge tests described in Chapter 2. Individual adaptability to change can be measured by paper-and-pencil tests as well as by simulated exercises.

The amount that an organization invests in adapting assessment centers to deal with changing needs will be a small fraction of the eventual costs of wrong decisions made in placing professionals in positions of responsibility. By reducing the possibility that incompetent individuals will rise very far in the organization, the so-called Peter Principle need not become a problem.

Although assessment centers have been used primarily for the selection of managerial manpower from nonsupervisory levels, there is no reason why the approach cannot be extended to determine the appropriate placement and transfer of professionals into nonmanagerial or staff positions. Such an extension might be useful in organizations with a "dual ladder" of advancement that is intended to allow promotions along professional as well as managerial career paths. If an appropriate combination of exercises, tests, and interviews is developed, the predispositions of professionals toward obsolescence can be determined by assessing the behavior, knowledge, and skills necessary for successfully adapting to future organizational demands. Not only can assessment centers be utilized for improving professional promotion and transfer decisions but each professional's training and development needs can be identified in order to design individualized updating programs. In fact, assessment, followed up with feedback sessions, has been of great value in promoting self-development as well as in creating more realistic and positive self-concepts. By focusing on the improvement of professional placement, development, and updating, assessment centers can help bring the problem of obsolescence under organizational control.

MANAGEMENT BY OBJECTIVES

Management by objectives (MBO) [6] has been suggested as a means of overcoming the negative effects of traditional performance appraisals by emphasizing the developmental aspects: the supervisor counsels and coaches subordinates who participate directly in establishing relevant goals. MBO was first described as a management method in the mid-1950s, and in a relatively short time it has been adopted by a wide variety of organizations. In recent years, MBO has been recommended as a technique for preventing obsolescence among organizational professionals. That becomes quite understandable upon an examination of the following aspects of MBO that are relevant to stimulating self-development and competence:

1. Challenging and realistic goals that satisfy the needs of both the individual and the organization are established by the professional in consultation with his manager. Participation by professionals in directing their job and career development in response to their own needs should be intrinsically motivating toward goal attainment. Since professionals generally desire difficult goals that they set for themselves, they will be strongly committed to attaining them. In fact, the greater the influence that professionals are allowed in establishing their goals in the MBO process, the more likely they are to become highly competent.

2. Instead of traits and personal characteristics, actual job behavior and the attainment of specific objectives are evaluated objectively and constructively. For example, a professional's effectiveness in completing a project or in learning a new method is appraised, not his loyalty to the organization or his personality traits.

3. There is a focus on future performance and development, and past behavior is evaluated primarily to help attain future improvement. Since past failures are not emphasized, defensive behavior is reduced. Short-range goals to be reached within a specified time frame are determined relevant to job objectives. Longer-range goals of professional development may be established to create expertise in emerging areas to

prevent obsolescence. In this manner, personalized self-development programs that satisfy both individual and organizational needs can be agreed upon by the professional and his manager.

4. Performance and development are compared with the objectives the individuals had set for themselves rather than with the attainment of their peers. Consequently, there is a chance for everyone to feel a sense of accomplishment and growth, which is likely to lead to an improved self-concept. Older professionals are not compared with their younger colleagues, but rather are evaluated on attainments relative to their own goals. Consequently, increasing age need not be associated with lack of goal achievement, and older professionals can maintain their development and avoid obsolescence.

5. Performance review sessions should be scheduled frequently to allow managers to provide feedback for subordinates. Professionals should carry out a self-review of their success in attaining objectives before bringing their deficiencies to the attention of their manager for advice and counseling as to how they can make improvements. Self-appraisal is likely to be effective, since the primary goal of MBO is self-development. This should eliminate the problem of defensive reactions to criticism originating from the superior. If some professionals have low self-esteem, frequent feedback with minimal criticism from superiors is likely to be helpful in motivating them toward higher goal attainment.

6. At each review session, long-range and more immediate goals can be revised and new goals can be added to provide for changing individual and organizational needs. This results in a continuous feedback that can challenge professionals and stimulate their self-development. Such a goal-directed approach will help professionals and their managers to bring updating programs more into line with long-range organizational and individual needs.

7. Not only should the effort expended in self-development be intrinsically rewarding, but there should be an organiza-

tional reward system that reinforces updating efforts. Evaluations of goal attainment obtained during the appraisal interview between the professional and his manager can lead to greater opportunities to utilize newly acquired knowledge and skills as well as increased responsibility. This will allow the professional to demonstrate improved competence and job performance—which, in turn, can be reinforced by more tangible rewards such as salary increases and promotions. Such a procedure should stimulate career growth, enhance the professional's self-concept, and minimize anxiety and insecurity resulting from the threat of obsolescence.

Although MBO can be an effective way to enhance the development of professionals, it appears that most managers neglect career counseling of their subordinates. It is possible that many managers do not feel capable of providing effective counseling and coaching. Although this shortcoming may be partially overcome by training in counseling techniques, some problems which affect the professional's job performance and career development cannot be handled adequately by the manager. In such cases the assistance of a professional career counselor would be required.

CAREER COUNSELING

Career counseling should be provided by someone who is not only an expert on career development in the organization but is also competent to handle personal problems such as those resulting from the mid-career crisis.[7] The professional should be able to utilize the services of such a counselor on a self-referral basis. By providing competent counseling to help their professionals cope with personal problems as well as career development, organizations can help reduce the deterioration in job performance and competence that often accompanies personal and career crises. Since one of the basic causes of obsolescence has been found to be a failure to plan career development, the counselor should provide guidance to the professional for alternate career paths in the organization. The counselor must be able to determine the type of development necessary for pursuing different career paths in the organization.

Changing career paths is a common occurrence among professionals, and it appears to be one of the most important reasons why professionals leave their jobs. Organizational career counselors must be equipped to handle the increasing trend toward multiple careers that is occurring among successful professionals as well as among those who have become obsolescent. In the not too distant future, it will become normal for professionals to undertake several different careers during their lifetimes. Counselors can help such individuals make appropriate career changes within the organization by assisting them in defining their goals and evaluating their strengths and weaknesses so they can make more realistic career decisions.

Career path counseling is sometimes carried out informally by the professional's immediate supervisor or his manager. Very often managers have to deal with the problem of improper placement that can occur among newly hired as well as among experienced professionals. An example of such a frustrating counseling problem, which could have been avoided by proper selection and placement, is provided by the following description of a manager's experience with a newly hired engineer:

> He didn't have . . . what I would have considered at that time the rudiments of electrical engineering. . . . I tried personally to counsel [him] that he should give serious thought to alternatives because of the terrific deficiency he had at that level. My manager also tried to counsel him, but the kid was bent on being an engineer. . . . In the end, he was let go from the company. He just wouldn't channel himself into anything else. So, obsolescence, in my mind, comes about [because] the man wouldn't change, not [because] he couldn't. He could become a buyer . . . or he could have become maybe even a manager in manufacturing. . . . The young graduate couldn't cope with the engineer's job that he tried to do. They tried again to kind of match the job to him within

the framework that generally was set. He wouldn't take the job we offered.

This case illustrates the need for career counseling to be integrated into the placement process as soon as the professional is inducted into the organization. That most organizations do not provide for such career path counseling may result in untold losses of highly qualified professionals who separate from their organizations to seek career fulfillment elsewhere. Therefore, it would appear that career path counseling is a necessary part of any comprehensive program for developing an organization's human resources and bring obsolescence under control. The only type of formal counseling many organizations do provide is preretirement counseling, later in the career, to ease the older professionals into their new role as retirees. The importance of retirement in the professional career requires a more complete discussion.

Retirement: A Need for Flexible Policies

As one response to the problem of obsolescence among older professionals, organizations are increasingly going the route of mandatory retirement prior to age 65.[8] For example, forced retirement for executives at age 60 has been adopted by several major corporations. This is an easy solution, since it eliminates the need to make retirement decisions on an individual basis. However, as should be obvious from the discussion of aging in Chapter 3, not all professionals become obsolescent with increasing age. Those who possess the appropriate ability, motivation, and personality makeup stand an excellent chance of successfully resisting obsolescence later in their careers, and they may in fact be more valuable to the organization as a result of their accumulated experience.

Yet if the current trend in lowering the mandatory retirement age continues, it is not too far-fetched that professionals may be put on the shelf well before they reach their sixtieth year. This can initiate a self-fulfilling prophecy, since it will create the conditions for problems of obsolescence to emerge at an even earlier age. Professionals who are approaching a mandatory retirement age will often not receive promotions even though deserved, will have limited opportunities to learn about new developments in their fields even if they have the necessary abilities, and may be shunted to dead-end jobs where any self-motivation to avoid obsolescence will soon become nonexistent.

As a result of the anxiety generated by such limitations on their career development, professionals in their preretirement period will concentrate their efforts on satisfying their security rather than their growth needs. In fact, managers in their preretirement period derive their job satisfaction primarily from attaining security goals, whereas previously that satisfaction came from goals that gratified growth needs. Since organizations generally do not give older professionals the opportunity to gratify their growth needs, those individuals have no choice but to limit their self-development and concentrate on protecting their positions in the organization until they retire. The image of older professionals sitting back and waiting for retirement further reinforces the organization's argument in favor of an earlier mandatory retirement age.

Organizational policy generally does not take into consideration individual differences when it comes to retirement. For most professionals work is an integral, if not a central, part of the self-concept, and that explains why so many professionals tend to reject early retirement. Studies indicate that almost nine out of ten professionals of preretirement age would prefer to work even if they were made financially secure by receiving money not to work. Despite this fact, some four out of five professionals are retired involuntarily.

The strong need to work felt by older professionals is further supported by a study of M.B.A. graduates between the ages of 66 and 82. Despite their advanced age, one out of four of these professionals was still actively engaged in full-time work; and of those who were retired, half had reached that status involuntarily. Almost half of those still working planned never to retire. Reasons for continuing to work included such statements as "I would go *nuts* if I retired" and "Why should anyone want to retire when you can have so much fun working?" [9] Perhaps more revealing are the following comments, by some who stopped working, about the principal difficulties they experienced in retirement: [10]

> "[Need] to overcome the compulsion or inner drive to work."
> "Feeling of not being productive."
> "Reluctance to quit work."
> "Lack of sense of accomplishment."
> "Not as much mental stimulus as when working."
> "Erosion of exercise of decision-making policies tends to diminish self-respect."

The effects of such difficulties brought on by forced retirement can be highly destructive to the individual. Life insurance companies have found that men in good health who are forced to retire at age 65 do not live to the age they were expected to reach, whereas those who continue working beyond 65 live longer than expected. This premature mortality may be related to the trauma accompanying the feelings of uselessness that can result from early forced retirement.

Given the expressed need to continue working, it is not surprising that many professionals are in favor of a flexible retirement policy without a mandatory retirement age. Such a flexible policy can base retirement decisions, at least in part, on the degree to which a professional is obsolescent and whether or not anti-obsolescence measures would be effective in each individual case. This approach is reflected in the following suggestion by a professional about to be retired:

> Retirement should be based on the individual's ability to perform rather than on an arbitrary chronological principle . . . instead of being automatic, both parties should have a choice. Perhaps it will be advisable to test the individual's intellectual ability and professional competence and then determine whether he may go on.[11]

Older professionals who remain competent and up to date in their fields should not have to undergo the anxiety of approaching forced retirement. If competent professionals desire to remain with the organization regardless of their age, opportunities for their further development and growth should be provided. The expertise of the older professional can be utilized in such activities as training and development of younger professionals, investigating broad problem areas that are important to the organization's long-range goals, and serving as internal consultants. Not only will the organization be able to benefit from the longer service of its more competent and experienced professionals, but without mandatory retirement threatening them, fewer professionals are likely to slow down their development and become obsolescent when they reach middle age. Compulsory retirement of competent professionals entails a substantial loss to the organization's investment in its professional manpower resources. This problem is likely to be critical in the future, since the low birth rate in the United States portends an increasingly elderly population that may have to be utilized productively rather than removed from the labor force as is the current practice.

On the other hand, professionals who do become obsolescent can be retired at an earlier age, and it is quite possible that they would desire early retirement. Studies have shown that those who have a strong professional identification tend to reject early retirement, whereas those who desire to change their profession favor early retirement. The desire for career change may be a result of obsolescence, and management would be wise to facilitate the early retirement of such professionals provided that a redirection of their careers in the organization proves unfeasible. Although some organizations retire their obsolescent professionals at age 50, that practice should be applied by using a flexible, as opposed to a fixed, retirement age.

Obsolescent individuals may welcome early retirement as an opportunity either for changing their careers or for participating in leisure activities. Attaining these goals may be more intrinsically satisfying to their needs than remaining as marginal contributors in their organizations would be. It would certainly provide obsolescent professionals with an easy method for removing the anxiety engendered by their lack of further goal achievement in their organizational careers.

Instituting such a policy of flexible retirement should not be difficult, since over nine out of ten American organizations already allow early retirement and almost half of those who retire do so before they reach the mandatory age. Moreover, most companies offer preretirement counseling programs, which can be expanded to focus on identifying obsolescent professionals and counseling them for early retirement. Effective early retirement counseling should reduce resistance to retiring, which is quite common. A flexible policy of retirement that eliminates the deadwood in the organization also opens up positions for the younger, more competent professionals who might otherwise become frustrated with their lack of advancement and leave the organization.

Older obsolescent professionals can be encouraged to retire early by providing them with full or partial pension payments. More than half of U.S. corporations already provide such financial incentives. A related approach to reducing the number of obsolescent professionals is to facilitate the use of portable pension vesting rights. Such rights are often lost if employees leave or are dismissed from their organizations. The obsolescent older professional is likely to be very security conscious and consequently more likely to remain in the same organization in order not to lose his pension rights. However, providing portable pensions will help encourage greater turnover of the less competent professionals.

Integrating Personnel Practices

In this chapter I have suggested a variety of personnel techniques which can capitalize on differences in personal characteristics to bring obsolescence under organizational control. As the reader may have noted, the techniques discussed are relevant to stimulating development during different career stages as follows: (1) Methods of selection and placement determine the very crucial first job experience. (2) Assessment centers, MBO, and counseling are most relevant for professional development and adjustment to change during the subsequent career. (3) Finally, flexible retirement policies can have a crucial effect on coping with the problems that occur toward the end of the professional career. In order for such approaches to be applied successfully in the control of obsolescence, organizations will have to become more adept at predicting future professional job requirements. This may be accomplished by utilizing techniques such as technological, manpower, and job forecasting. It will also be necessary to develop counselors and assessors who not only are expert in judging people but also are knowledgeable about the demands of the environments in which professionals will work.

Although any one of the approaches suggested in this chapter should have some effect on diminishing obsolescence, an overall organizational commitment to a total, rather than a piecemeal, attack on the problem will have the greatest effect on maintaining a high level of competence among professional employees. Such a total commitment requires an integration of all personnel policies and practices with the objective of creating a professional workforce that is both competent and highly adaptable to change.

Clearly, other anti-obsolescence techniques besides those already described are available to organizations. Whereas the approaches discussed thus far have focused on responding to individual differences among professionals, the next chapter will deal with the organizational work environment and how it can be utilized to control obsolescence.

Chapter 5

The Work Environment
and Job Design

ALTHOUGH ORGANIZATIONS can attempt to control obsolescence by focusing on the individual strengths and weaknesses of their professionals through appropriate selection, placement, assessment, and counseling procedures, their efforts are doomed to failure unless the environment in which their professionals work encourages their keeping up to date. This fact was recognized by the behavioral scientists at the First Conference on Occupational Obsolescence, who not only felt "that the characteristics of the environment and the interaction of the environment and the individual are important considerations" [1] but also that "the environmental factors in obsolescence are more important than the individual factors." [2] That holds much promise for organizations, because it should be easier to modify the work environment than to effect a direct change in the individual characteristics of professionals. In fact, it appears that the nature and intensity of the environmental demands experienced during the adult years may enhance the development or deterioration of even such relatively stable individual traits as intellectual abilities.[3]

In light of this, it is not too far-fetched to expect that the work environment plays *the* crucial role in determining the degree to which obsolescence occurs with increasing age. In this chapter we will examine some aspects of the work environment which encourage keeping up to date and see how techniques of job design can be used to keep obsolescence in check.

Work Challenge and Utilization

As was discussed in Chapter 3, one of the most important goals of professionals, if not *the* most important goal, is to do challenging work. Yet an overwhelming majority of professionals feel that they are not challenged, because their abilities, knowledge, and skills are poorly utilized by their organizations. Thwarting professionals' very strong growth needs by denying them an opportunity to do challenging work results not only in lower job satisfaction and morale but also in fewer professional contributions, poorer job performance, and increased turnover. The apparently all-pervasive effect of work challenge on the development of professionals occurs quite early in the career and involves several important dimensions.

THE CRITICAL FIRST-JOB EXPERIENCE

Accumulating evidence has consistently demonstrated that the type of work to which professionals are assigned during the first year or two of their initial job experience has long-lasting effects on later job success and career development. The most clear-cut support for the crucial importance of first-job experience is provided by the Bell System's ambitious long-term management progress study.[4] The study found that the challenge and demands experienced during the first year of work by newly hired college graduates tended to have a greater influence on eventual performance and career success than did the challenge and demands of succeeding years.

Work challenge involved the degree to which the new managers were expected to utilize their knowledge and skills, use new methods, solve novel problems, apply their learning capacity, become involved in self-development, commit their time and energy, demonstrate initiative, and so on. Clearly, such expectations will help stimulate the growth of the young managers; conversely, managers with limited work challenge are likely to become frustrated, reduce their aspirations, or perhaps even leave the organization to obtain challenging jobs elsewhere. The results of the Bell System's management progress study revealed such outcomes, as is clear from the following findings:

- Of those who voluntarily left the company early in their careers, 55 percent did so because of unchallenging work, the most frequently mentioned reason for terminating.
- Of those who had been highly challenged by their early work experiences, 70 percent increased in their motivation to achieve, compared with only 8 percent of those who had unchallenging assignments.
- There was an increase in concern for really accomplishing something, as distinct from advancement or making more money, among those who experienced challenging jobs early in their career, whereas there was a decrease in desire for accomplishment among those who experienced low initial work challenge.

In general, college graduates who were assigned to more challenging work showed positive changes in attitudes and motivation as they progressed through their careers. The Bell System findings strongly suggest that, from the very outset of their careers, some professionals are challenged toward an upward spiral in their development, whereas those who are not challenged tend to stagnate or deteriorate if they remain in the unchallenging work environment.

The above results are not unique to either the Bell System or managers. For instance, studies of engineers in several organizations have demonstrated that being initially assigned to work which demands utilization of technical knowledge and skills is significantly associated with job performance, professional contributions, and competence in the subsequent career.[5] Early work challenge affected later job and professional success, regardless of individual differences in ability and interest. However, the greatest effect of being assigned to challenging work occurred among those professionals who were more capable from the outset. This was a clear demonstration of how professional career development and success occur when individuals have the appropriate abilities and the work environment demands utilization of those abilities.

The discouraging fact is that too frequently organizations do not assign new professionals immediately to permanent and realistically challenging assignments in which they can demonstrate their ability and make important contributions. Initial training programs that may involve exposure to the organization via job rotation should be as short as possible, if they are necessary. The young professional does not want to sit around and observe; he is anxious to show what he can do.

However, management may be unwilling to risk giving untried professionals immediate responsibility, preferring to observe them first in temporary tasks in which they cannot seriously affect the organization and then gradually ease them into more responsible permanent jobs. In addition, it is not an easy matter to make jobs more challenging, and organizations may feel that it is not worth the effort. That is an extremely short-sighted view, since providing challenging work to new professionals can pay off in many ways that could greatly outweigh the resources allocated to upgrade the first-job experience.

For example, one organization had to hire 120 new employees each year so that there would be 20 by the end of the year.[6] Its management felt that the high turnover rate was a result of the lack of job challenge provided to the new hires. Therefore, the following year it concentrated on upgrading the entry-level jobs and hired only 30 instead of 120 new employees. The increased challenge paid off, since not only were 25 remaining at the end of the first year but their performance was far better than that of new hires in preceding years.

The effects of work challenge may be another demonstration

of the self-fulfilling prophecy: people perform in the way they are expected to perform. Professionals who are expected to utilize their knowledge and skills in challenging first-work assignments will be stimulated to good job performance and increased competence quite early in their careers. This should, in turn, generate organizational rewards including increased responsibility and more challenging work assignments in a continuous process of reinforcement throughout their careers. Since this process is most effective when it is initiated at the outset of the career, organizations should attempt to increase the challenge and stimulation provided by the first-job experience. Therefore, by controlling the initial job assignments, management can have a powerful influence in enhancing their professionals' contributions, job successes, and career development.

Dimensions of Utilization

Utilization of knowledge and skills is an important aspect of work challenge and has been found to be strongly related to obsolescence. Two relatively independent dimensions of utilization have been identified.[7] They are misutilization and underutilization.

MISUTILIZATION

Perhaps the most important type of utilization relevant to obsolescence is what has been labeled "misutilization" of knowledge and skills. It is reported to be widespread among professionals. Misutilization is greatest when professionals experience light intellectual demands on their jobs together with heavy time pressure. Misutilization results from the professionals' working under time pressure at assignments so routine that they could and should be done by clerical personnel or by technicians. Typical of misutilization is the following complaint by an engineer: "Now many people are *expected* to work 52 or more hours a week!!! In my department there are three engineers and two non-exempt technicians doing identical work. If the engineers try to get the technicians to do any routine paper work, there is a major battle." [8]

Frequently professionals will cite misutilization as a major contributor to their obsolescence. Indeed, the two most important causes of obsolescence have been identified by professionals as follows: [9]

- · Work assignments that do not require knowledge of the latest developments.
- · The pressure of schedule demands that leave no time or energy for study.

In order to demonstrate the relationship between misutilization and obsolescence, data obtained from two independent engineering development laboratories are presented in Figure

FIGURE 7   Relationship between engineers' keeping up with new developments and perceived misutilization in their work at two laboratories.

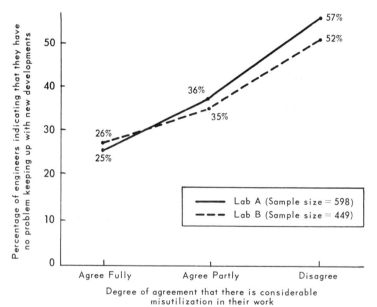

7. From these data it appears that three out of four of those who report considerable misutilization in their work have a problem in keeping up with new developments. On the other hand, over half of those who feel that misutilization is not a problem report having no trouble keeping up to date. In essence, professionals can avoid obsolescence to the extent that they are required to use their knowledge and skills. Being assigned to work which does not utilize professional abilities, knowledge, and skills may lead either to misutilization or to what has been identified as underutilization.

UNDERUTILIZATION

Underutilization is similar to misutilization in that it involves only light intellectual demands on the job, but the under-utilized professional has light rather than heavy time demands. This situation apparently occurs most frequently during the crucial early stage of the professional's career, as evidenced by the following comment by a newly hired college graduate:

> Due to being a new employee fresh from college, I am quite disturbed that I have been left to "entertain" myself and have been assigned very little work. I realize that a new employee cannot expect to be assigned to a project of which he knows nothing, but I do feel that it is at this point in his career with the company that he is forming his first real opinions about the company. I have had days in which the only relief from boredom was to spend time in the library, which is informative, but does nothing to introduce me to my job.[10]

As should be clear from this comment, underutilization is a great danger to the new employee's development because the job itself does not provide any challenge. Despite the fact that underutilization may inhibit career development, obsolescence may not occur as readily as it would if the professional were misutilized. Nevertheless, either can contribute to obsolescence. The underutilized professional quoted above is not intellectually stimulated by his job, but he does have the time to keep informed. If he decides to remain in the organization and continues to be underutilized, he may have to resort to taking continuing-education courses in order to keep up to date. However, if this new college graduate does not have the initiative to keep abreast of new developments, his professional knowledge and skills will gradually decay and he will be well on his way to becoming obsolescent.

Problems of utilization are likely to be exacerbated in the near future, since projections show that the rapid growth in the numbers of college-educated workers will force an increasing percentage of them into jobs that do not utilize their ability, knowledge, and skills. The effects of both misutilization and underutilization can be avoided by providing professionals with intellectually demanding job assignments combined with time pressure. Although among professionals job satisfaction is strongly associated with the intellectual demands of work, some increase in job satisfaction also accompanies increases in time pressure. In fact, there is clear evidence that time pressure, as well as demands for quality, plays important roles in attaining both individual and organizational goals.[11] Not only do professionals desire time pressure, but when the pressure they experience is too low, their performance suffers. This flies in the face of management folklore that advocates a relaxed environment as necessary for professional development. It should be noted, however, that too much time pressure may ultimately be counterproductive, because long-term stress associated with time schedules can have detrimental effects on physical and mental health.

Nevertheless, if professionals participate in setting their own work goals, including realistic time schedules needed to reach those goals, problems resulting from too much stress are likely to be diminished. That is clearly another argument in favor of the management-by-objectives approach to goal setting discussed in Chapter 4. With such an approach, organizations need not be afraid to encourage the setting of deadlines among their professionals. But this participation will be effective in controlling obsolescence only to the extent that the work is intellectually demanding.

Thus far, we have examined two aspects of work challenge that affect obsolescence: (1) intellectual demands and (2) time pressure. We will now turn to a third dimension of work challenge that is perhaps even more intimately connected with obsolescence—change.

Dynamic Versus Stable Environments

Although work environments that are impacted by change might be expected to have the greatest problems in dealing with obsolescence, they actually tend to produce the lowest numbers of obsolescent professionals.[12] For instance, it has been demonstrated that engineers who are employed in industries characterized by rapid technological change acquire a greater amount of new knowledge than do those who work in less dynamic environments. The incidence of obsolescence is also less of a problem among managers in companies that have had a high average annual growth rate.

On closer examination, these findings are not as paradoxical as they might first appear, especially if they are viewed in terms of the challenge created by the work environment. Professionals employed in industries in which change has been an integral part of organizational life, such as electronics and computers, have been stimulated to stay up to date—their environments have demanded it. This situation is depicted by a middle manager working in the computer industry:

> We are faced continuously with the problem of starting off in a new area in which the people frequently involved have very little, if any, prior knowledge of the area. . . . We find quite generally in a short period of time that the people can acquire sufficient knowledge in that area and can compete on an equal footing with so-called experts. . . . We have a situation where every year or two, in any given project, the people are technically obsolete in [the] sense of the area that they have been working in no longer being applicable to their current job.

The greatest difficulties are likely to occur among professionals in stable industries, in which a sudden change may be quite traumatic to those who previously had not experienced much change. The automobile industry is a good example. Having grown accustomed to a product line that has experienced minor change during the years, the automotive industry has found it extremely difficult to adjust to the new technological requirements made necessary by stringent government standards. The aerospace industry also has been thrown into turmoil, as a result of cutbacks in federal government funds. Aerospace professionals were working on unique products in a relatively secure environment that was insulated to a large degree from the competition of the consumer marketplace. They have had great difficulty in adjusting to the changes involved in switching to more consumer-oriented product lines that require different design, manufacturing, marketing, and pricing criteria. A good example of this problem is the difficulty experienced by Rohr Industries, Inc., a large aerospace subcontractor that has turned to producing mass-rapid-transit systems. Rohr's chairman and chief executive, Burt F. Raynes, did not mince words when he described the effect of the sudden change on his organization: "It was bloody—that's the right word for it, bloody. You had to change the way people think and that's not easy. It takes a stick of intellectual dynamite to bust them loose from the past. It was traumatic as hell, on people, on the company." [13]

Even within dynamic industries, professionals can be assigned to work roles that can range from being relatively stable to requiring frequent changes in job assignments. The change that professionals experience in their work roles has an influence on their obsolescence over and above that of the types of organizations in which they are employed.

CHANGES IN JOB ASSIGNMENTS

There is evidence that professionals who have been exposed to frequent job assignments during their career can more easily adapt to change and become up to date. This phenomenon is described by a middle manager working in a dynamic environment in the computer industry:

> If the point is reached in a particular type of facility, where you have a very stable environment over a long period of time, where the job that the man is doing gets gradually degraded to one of repetition or no challenges and so on, and this becomes established over a period of time, then I can see that when faced with a change this would be a traumatic experience and he may or may not be able to cope with it. . . .
>
> Having had a background of change does, I think, contribute greatly to his potential up-to-dateness, if you like, or the mental willingness to become up-to-date. If you've never had the background of change, then it's a frightening prospect to be faced with something which seems to be so strange and new. If you have had the experience of change, what you realize after a period of time is that it isn't so new, it isn't so different. What may be different is the vocabulary and the terminology and a few little gimmicks, but basically there are very few things that are different.

The manager continues by describing his own ability to adapt to changing job requirements and how it was developed during his career.

> If the job is within my capabilities, I will be able to adapt to it. I will be able to adjust to acquire whatever knowledge that is specific to it in a short enough period of time and do it in a proper fashion. . . . The first time that I made a change, I was very concerned. I was very worried and probably the second time, a little bit less. But as time has gone on, if anything, I may have gotten over-confident in my ability to make the change. . . . I may underestimate the amount of effort required, but I feel that I have been conditioned over these years for a change and it doesn't bother me. . . .
> To acquire and maintain in a conscious fashion [a] particular skill—you maintain it by using it.

The very perceptive insight of this middle manager makes it quite clear that being able to adjust to change successfully involves a learning process that requires experiencing change and acquiring confidence that one can successfully respond to the challenge of change and grow as a result of it. On the other hand, if the professional has been exposed to a stable, unchanging environment, he will be conditioned to expecting that stability to continue, and any major change may be threatening and will therefore be resisted.

There is rather clear-cut evidence that the longer professionals remain in the same job assignments, the less they feel their high-level growth needs are satisfied.[14] The danger to professionals of such immobility includes arrested development and deterioration of the capability to stay up to date. Of course, that is more likely to occur when the jobs are routine. In fact, it has been found that initiative drops precipitously with age for those in routine jobs, whereas it may increase among individuals in more demanding positions. It was explained that "being for a long period of time in a job where initiative is not required and even discouraged or disapproved of kills the expression of whatever capacity for initiative the person possesses. Being on a job where there are many and continuous opportunities to manifest initiative fosters it." [15]

The challenge provided by frequent job assignment changes is effective in keeping professional obsolescence at a minimum. In fact, data collected by the author demonstrate that providing different job assignments from the very beginning of the career is highly associated with staying professionally up to date in subsequent years.

It should be pointed out, however, that not all changes in job assignments help professionals keep up to date. For instance, being assigned to many jobs that are routine in nature would not provide challenge and would thereby tend to contribute to obsolescence. In addition, job assignments should last long enough for the professional to become proficient in the specialties required to perform the job effectively. This is clearly an argument *against* arbitrary and poorly planned job rotation, which often involves assignments that are not challenging and are of short duration.

CHANGING TO AN ADMINISTRATIVE CAREER:
A RESPONSE TO OBSOLESCENCE

As we saw in Chapter 4, moving to a new assignment can frequently represent a change in the professional's career path. Often such a change is sought by a professional who has become obsolescent in his field, and it frequently involves moving to an administrative or management position. As one manager explains:

> Very often in a few years a man will be ready for the technological wastebasket. . . . This is one of the reasons that they slide over into management. . . . Things are moving ahead so fast [technologically] that management is the only alternative to keep ahead. Management is a one-way door. It's almost impossible for an engineer to go back to the trade after having marked time in management for a few years.[16]

This type of impending career change necessitates careful assessment and counseling to determine which path would be most appropriate for the professional and the organization. Perhaps a job change to a position that is demanding in terms of administrative skills would be best for the obsolescent professional who does not want to remain in his field. A lack of ability and motivation to stay up to date may even exist at the beginning of the career. This frequently results in a desire to leave a specialist position for one in management. As a young engineer explains:

> I don't think that I am that well equipped technically— and I don't intend to be. I would like to be a leader. . . . I think the technical side scares you, and management is more glamorous. Dealing with people is more natural, normal. Technical knowledge is built up from scratch. It requires taking courses to keep up. You can read reports in the technical end only so long as you can understand the basic field, otherwise, it's incomprehensible.[17]

There is evidence that obsolescence can be both a cause and a consequence of job change during the career. One study that found this to be true explains "that recruitment into administration is from the ranks of those who have suffered deterioration of previously held knowledge and that such nontechnical duties foster further knowledge loss through disuse." [18] However, these results would most likely apply primarily to professionals who devote almost all of their time to administration and very little to their field of specialty. Managers who continue to utilize their professional knowledge and skills will tend to remain up to date. In fact, the immediate supervisors of specialists have been found to be somewhat more knowledgeable about newly emerging fields than their subordinates. This is encouraging, because it indicates that the most competent professionals are being rewarded with increased responsibility and promotions.

It is obvious from the evidence presented so far that obsolescence results in part from being assigned to jobs that are relatively stable and do not require different types of professional knowledge and skills. These types of assignments are typical and may result from an overemphasis on specialization.

SPECIALIZATION AND DIVERSITY

In this age of specialization, organizational professionals often become highly proficient in narrow job assignments. Contrary to the emphasis on specialization and division of labor in traditional management philosophy, there is a strong desire among many professionals to utilize their abilities in a broad field of interest rather than in a specialized area. Professionals who have a wide grasp of important new fields rather than a thorough knowledge of narrow specialties have been found to make greater contributions to both their organization and their professions. This is particularly true among older professionals. Having a diversity of specializations rather than only one not only enhances a professional's usefulness to the organization but also stimulates a wide range of professional contributions. Being assigned to a narrow area over a long period of time can lead to an inability to perform other parts of the job. That can be seen from the following description of the reason why a manager felt one of his subordinates was obsolescent:

> His failure to be able to follow through [on a] problem to its obvious conclusion. . . . He went for a long time not having to do this. . . . He lost the knack to do it or lost the ambition to do it. I think they are both tied up in this particular case. He is no longer capable of doing it. . . . He reached this stage through having a narrow part of a total problem and always having that narrow part of the total problem for too long a period of time. . . . He fell down on the previous assignment in a similar situation.

Not surprisingly, many professionals feel that obsolescence is likely to occur when the work is so specialized that the broader base of knowledge is unused and forgotten. It has been found that professionals become obsolescent

> . . . when they are allowed to settle complacently in a narrow area that has not been evolving very rapidly. Their complacency seems to prevent their anticipating or participating in the radical developments that may be about to unfold in their areas, and their routine involvement in their development seems to dull any desire to acquaint themselves with these developments, once they have occurred.[19]

That is substantiated by the fact that the single most important stimulation for professional development and growth is on-the-job problem solving that often requires a diversity of challenging work assignments. This is indicated in statements such as the following:[20]

- "The thing that keeps me up-to-date is that I have an opportunity to become involved in a variety of interesting projects and assignments."
- "If I keep getting projects closely related to my own specialty, I find that I get very narrow. . . . I really learn when I have a chance to get involved in projects outside my area of specialization."

However, as one study has found, professionals who continually face a diversity of new problems "are never allowed to settle comfortably into a narrow niche, and although they may be nagged by a sense of never having fully mastered any project, they are *forced* to maintain a competency in several allied fields simultaneously." [21]

It becomes very clear that obsolescence is very much a result of how professionals' work is organized. What is rather disconcerting, however, is that most professionals are assigned to positions that do not require utilization of the wide breadth of their abilities, knowledge, and skills. Even among professionals in executive roles, which should provide the greatest diversity, only somewhat over half (54 percent) report that their positions involve very few routine activities.

Other organizational roles are even more restrictive. A Stanford Research Institute report [22] concludes that only about 15 percent of technical manpower is required to be in the forefront of knowledge and an additional 30 percent is required to maintain a high degree of competence. What, then, happens to the remaining 55 percent of the professionals? It has been suggested that they should be reasonably up to date only in their job assignments, which may require working on what have been termed "formatted tasks." [23] This accords with the conclusion of one researcher, whose estimates of utilization among engineers are remarkably similar to the above data:

> *The engineering content of most engineering-related jobs is not very high.* Most engineers work on "formatted tasks," that may have a high skill content and that place emphasis on know-how. But their engineering-related aspects have a high degree of near-repetitiveness which demands little in terms of science-based knowledge or in terms of being up-to-date. . . . 50–60% of engineers perform almost entirely formatted tasks. Their engineering underpinnings erode with age and misuse. They become rapidly obsolete and are saved only because so much engineering does not change while the overall technology advances.[24]

Obviously, professionals who have become highly specialized in doing formatted tasks may have to face the specter of obsolescence if they are required to switch to a different specialty requiring knowledge and skills that they have either not maintained or not developed.

Since the main contributor to obsolescence is the work itself and how it is organized, management can reorganize the professional's jobs in order to stimulate the utilization of knowledge and skills and instill a desire to stay abreast of new developments. A reorganization of work can be attained by using such techniques as job design and enrichment.

Job Design and Enrichment

The technique of job enrichment is rapidly becoming one of the management fads of the 1970s. The basic approach of enrichment has been around for decades in the form of job design, but its sudden popularity is probably a result of the proselytizing efforts of growth-oriented organizational psychologists coming at a time when the expectations and aspirations of the American labor force are increasingly oriented toward achievement and growth. Industrial corporations are asking how to deal with the problem of worker alienation, particularly among the younger, more educated employees, and the answer provided them is job enrichment.

The reason for this will become clear if we examine what job enrichment attempts to do and how it relates to satisfying the needs of different occupational groups. There are two types of change that enrichment attempts to accomplish by redesigning jobs:

1. *Job content changes,* which add new job requirements involving greater variety and challenge. This is sometimes referred to as "vertical loading" of the job as opposed to "horizontal loading." The latter merely adds more of the same kind of content, as is often true of job enlargement.

2. *Increase in decision-making responsibility,* which allows employees to determine how their jobs should be carried out and makes individuals more responsible and accountable for their work.

By increasing challenge and responsibility in jobs, enrichment also is supposed to provide greater opportunities for individual achievement, recognition, advancement, and growth. The very legitimate question has been asked whether all employees desire challenge and responsibility in their work. The answer is probably that not all do, at least among nonprofessional workers, but the enrichment goals are clearly those for which professionals are striving. In practice, however, job enrichment has been applied primarily to the more structured types of work carried out by nonprofessional, frequently unskilled or semiskilled employees. It is clearly easier to enrich jobs that are limited in content and responsibility, but we have already seen that many professionals also work on routine, repetitive jobs in which there may be limited utilization of their abilities, knowledge, and skills as well as decision-making responsibility. Professionals, then, are prime candidates for job enrichment efforts. Job enrichment for professionals is different from enrichment for other workers, since it not only can tap an existing motivational potential but can also be used to fight obsolescence and enhance professional career development. This is elaborated in the following analysis:

> Job enrichment means something different for the professional worker than it does for, say, clerical workers. Job enrichment applied to nonprofessional, clerical jobs is essentially a motivational technique. The objective is to increase the task involvement of people alienated from their work. . . . The difficulty [for professionals] centers on a surplus of motivation, a desire to do more. . . .
>
> Thus, the aim of job enrichment in professional organizations is not one of reconstituting tasks to enhance motivation, but one of using the motivation that is already there. . . . [This] motivation lies as much in the next job—moving on to bigger and better things—as it does in the present one. This is why

the opportunity to learn and to develop new skills must be a salient feature of any program for job enrichment.[25]

Since job enrichment has been applied mostly to highly routine nonprofessional jobs, we may naturally ask how the relatively more complex professional-level jobs can be redesigned. Fortunately, there have been a handful of attempts to apply the techniques of job design and enrichment at the professional level. Different approaches have been used, and they will illustrate how the job itself can be redesigned to utilize the knowledge and skills of professionals.

One approach, used by the Autonetics Division of North American Rockwell Corporation,[26] begins with an analysis to determine the specific tasks performed in a particular professional job to meet the assigned objectives. The end product of the task analysis is a detailed list of the job tasks. Then the skill requirements of each task are rated by the professionals, their managers, and personnel specialists. A sample rating scale for quality engineers is illustrated in Table 3. In addition, each task is rated on the amount of incentive it has for the professional—for example, how much personal satisfaction

TABLE 3   Task skill-level scale.

LEVEL	DEFINITION
A	Requires the skills and knowledge of a quality engineer.
B	Can be adequately performed by a quality technician under the close direction of a quality engineer.
C	Can be adequately performed by a quality technician under little or no supervision.
D	Can be adequately performed by a clerk under the direction of a quality engineer.
E	Not a legitimate quality engineering task.

SOURCE: D. Harris and F. Chaney, "Human Factors in Quality Assurance," P7-2787/501, Autonetics Division of North American Rockwell, Anaheim, Calif., November 2, 1967, p. 21. With permission of Rockwell International, Electronics Group.

completing the task provides. Finally, the amount of time the professional spends at each task is determined.

An analysis of how effectively the skills of engineers were being utilized in quality engineering tasks revealed that these professionals were spending 51 percent of their time on tasks requiring the highest level of knowledge and skills. Since the engineers were already using a relatively high proportion of their time on tasks that were high in motivational value, the emphasis for the job design was to maximize utilization of professional knowledge and skills, rather than try to increase the number of high-incentive tasks. It was determined that 22 out of a total of 44 tasks performed by the engineers could be carried out by technicians. Accordingly, technicians were transferred from another part of the organization, where they had been performing five of the required tasks. During a period of four months, the technicians gradually assumed more responsibility for their reassigned tasks and the amount of direction and guidance by the engineers was reduced. Simultaneously, the engineers were increasing the utilization of their expertise on professional-level work. After the reassignment of tasks, the engineers were spending two-thirds of their time on higher-level professional work, compared with about half of their time prior to the phase-in. These gains are illustrated in Figure 8, which shows the amount of time allotted to engineering and technician-level tasks before, during, and after the job redesign. As a result of job redesign, the technicians' skill utilization also was upgraded. That was an important spin-off from redesigning the professional jobs, since technicians also are commonly misutilized by being required to do clerical and submarginal tasks.

Typical job enrichment methods are generally not as elaborate or methodical as the preceding description of job redesign would imply. Although there may be a work flow analysis to identify the attributes of the job to be modified, the enrichment approach usually involves several levels of managers who generate ideas for enriching the job in an open brainstorming session. This often results in over a hundred suggestions, which are screened and then implemented.

Job enrichment techniques have been applied to professional and highly skilled jobs, and perhaps the most carefully implemented of such programs was carried out at Imperial Chemical Industries Limited and other companies in England.[27] The problems of utilization were evident in various professional jobs in those companies, particularly in the form of too much routine work or heavy time pressure. All jobs were enriched by increasing the technical, financial, and managerial responsibilities of the employees. Not only did increased productivity and job satisfaction result from the enrichment program but professional growth also took place, in the form of self-initiated training and development and increased expertise

FIGURE 8   Time spent on 22 technician and 22 quality-engineering tasks by quality engineers.

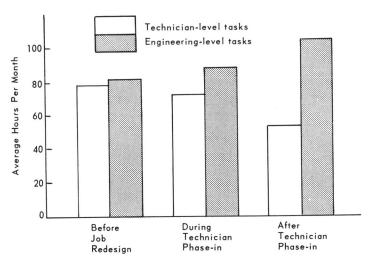

SOURCE: D. Harris and F. Chaney, "Human Factors in Quality Assurance," P7-2787/501, Autonetics Division of North American Rockwell, Anaheim, Calif., November 2, 1967, p. 21. With permission of Rockwell International, Electronics Group.

in a greater number of fields. Job enrichment appears to have had a positive "ecological" effect, since not only was there an improved utilization of professionals and their support staff but the supervisors of the professionals had their routine involvement reduced and were able to concentrate more on development.

The essence of job enrichment is that the organizational professional not only remains a specialist but becomes a manager as well. His responsibility is expanded so that he has control over a broader range of problems in his field. His influence is increased in decisions involving a support staff of technical and clerical personnel. It has been pointed out, however, that the success or failure of job enrichment for professionals may hinge on aspects of the work environment that are more encompassing than the job itself. There are organizational factors that can prevent the utilization and development of professionals even if job enrichment is attempted. A discussion of that problem is left for the next chapter, which focuses on the organizational climate and its effect on obsolescence.

WE HAVE SEEN that a lack of challenge in the work environment has a profound and long-lasting effect on the careers of professionals that contributes directly to rapid obsolescence. This lack of challenge results from the fact that the abilities, knowledge, and skills of professionals are not properly utilized. The problem appears as either (1) misutilization, doing routine work that lacks intellectual demands under heavy time pressure, or (2) underutilization, doing work that lacks both intellectual and time pressure. Lack of challenge is also associated with stable work environments and with being assigned to highly specialized but narrow jobs over a long period of time.

It is quite clear that obsolescence is, to a great degree, a result of poor organization of a professional's work. Consequently, management has the power to create jobs that discourage obsolescence. It can do so by applying techniques of job design and enrichment to professional jobs in order to attain the following:

1. Increased challenge of entry-level positions to stimulate career development from the very beginning.
2. Changes in job content to maximize the utilization of professional knowledge and skills.
3. Increased decision-making responsibility that provides greater influence over work-relevant human and financial resources, as well as in setting realistic deadlines for meeting work goals.
4. Periodic changes in job assignments that require the continual learning of new knowledge and skills to provide a steady stream of challenging work experiences.

Such changes as the preceding ones will act to stretch the capabilities of professionals. This process should be continual so that each time an individual has demonstrated that he has grown to a new dimension he is stretched again. In this manner, professional growth can be maintained throughout the career. However, just as the personnel techniques recommended to control obsolescence in Chapter 4 are useless if the work itself does not offer appropriate challenge, so attempts at job design and enrichment are impotent if the organizational climate does not encourage staying up to date. This is the next issue which we must consider.

Chapter 6

Organizational
Climate

THE TERM "organizational climate" has become almost a catch-all; it includes perceived attributes of the work environment determined by management and organizational practices that affect the motivation and behavior of employees. The provision of challenge through utilization of knowledge and skills is to some degree determined by the technology of the organization, as we have already seen. But organizational climate can also stimulate or stifle that utilization, as well as provide or deny less tangible motivational challenges that can affect career development.

If organizations are viewed as socio-technical systems, in accordance with the current vogue among organizational theorists, climate might be described as being generated largely by the "socio" part of the system (for example, by higher management). It has also been suggested that climate may be that aspect of the organizational environment which determines the productive output of the technical system. That interrelationship becomes more concrete in this chapter when we examine aspects of the organizational climate that have been identified as relevant to obsolescence. They include colleague interaction and communication, leadership style and expertise, and management policies, as well as their effects on organizational communication, influence, uncertainty, and rewards. We will also see how organizational change and development can be used to create a climate that discourages obsolescence.

Colleague Interaction and Communication

One aspect of organizational climate is created by the colleagues with whom the professional works. Interaction and communication with colleagues provide an important source of stimulation for keeping up with the latest developments.[1] However, the role of such communication in updating will vary with the particular professional group. For example, in management at all levels it has been found that discussion with company personnel is the most frequently used method of keeping up to date with new information. Technical professionals also find that on-the-job colleague interaction is one of the most important sources of stimulation in keeping themselves informed.

However, most of this personal communication appears to be related to on-the-job problem solving. One study has demonstrated that 39 percent of the information engineers receive purely for staying up to date comes from interpersonal communication, almost half of which is within their own organizations. Scientists receive only 14 percent of new information in this way, most of it from individuals employed outside their organization. For all technical professionals, however, reading appears to be the most important source of new information. Nevertheless, the frequency with which professionals are in contact with their most important colleagues is directly related to their job performance and professional contributions.

The way work groups are organized can also determine whether they serve to motivate professionals to gain new knowledge and skills. Working with people who have diverse backgrounds can stimulate professionals to read and learn about different specialties, as the following statement indicates: "It's tremendous when I get assigned to a project that forces me to work with people outside my own particular specialty, even outside my own discipline. . . . It's very broadening, and the exchange stimulates me to do a lot of reading." [2]

Not only does diversity in the composition of work groups help stimulate professionals to keep informed of new developments, but it may also be necessary to have at least one person in the group who serves as the so-called gatekeeper of new knowledge. The gatekeeper acts as an intermediary between the work group and the outside world to acquire information. In a sense, gatekeepers serve to link the organization to relevant external sources of information either by reading the published information or by making personal contacts outside the organization. The gatekeepers are generally the most competent and up-to-date professionals in their group. They help to maintain organizational vitality by staying in close contact with gatekeepers in other groups in the organization through an informal communication network. They therefore provide multiple paths for communication with the external world.

The length of time professionals work together in the same group appears to influence the stimulation provided by colleagues. For instance, interaction with colleagues and diversity of group members have been found to be effective in stimulating competence in both job and profession only when the professionals have not worked together for too long. After several years individuals who have worked closely together no longer provide the stimulation and novelty they had generated earlier. This would suggest that not only job assignments should be changed periodically but the composition of work groups as well.

However, organizations should be wary of attempting to motivate professionals to stay up to date by bringing specialists with new skills into existing groups without simultaneously encouraging the development of those skills among group members. A policy of infusing new skills into a work group exclusively by obtaining specialists from outside the group serves to increase the obsolescence of existing group members. Apparently, such a policy discourages development of new skills among the existing professionals in favor of bringing a specialist who possesses the skills into the group. It would appear that a combined strategy of requiring current group members to learn the new skills and bringing specialists possessing those skills into the work group would provide a double-barreled approach to updating.

The manager of the professional work group can play a crucial role in facilitating and stimulating interaction and communication as well as other climate factors that can help stifle obsolescence. Let us take a closer look at how the manager can affect his professional subordinates.

Leadership Style and Expertise

One of the most important influences on the behavior of professionals is the leadership style of the immediate manager.[3] Managers of professionals can affect individual and organizational performance by altering the climate within the group, which may in turn affect other parts of the organization. For example, it has been demonstrated that an autocratic leadership style can have long-range detrimental effects not only on the professional contributions and morale of subordinates directly under the autocratic manager's control but also on professionals working in the same environment under nonautocratic managers.

On the other hand, a permissive type of leadership style that provides absolute freedom for professionals to carry out work according to their own ideas does not necessarily stimulate contributions or improve performance. It may indeed be dysfunctional to the individual and the organization. That is illustrated by an experiment at Kimberly-Clark Corporation, where a group of professionals from diverse fields were given total freedom to work on what they wanted. The group had no defined responsibility for particular areas, and they were not subject to company rules and regulations. They were even provided with their own independent financial resources, laboratories, and machine shop.

Once they had complete freedom, were these professionals more satisfied and productive? On the contrary, as witness the description of what happened in the group according to one of the participants:

> Their anxiety rose and was manifested in such statements as "We aren't as free now as we were before." . . . Our anxiety rose to tremendous heights. However, as a group we came to the realization that we had to limit our freedom. This was true regardless of what we worked on. We finally learned that the very essence of our freedom was our ability to limit its scope.[4]

Giving complete freedom to those professionals resulted in continual arguments about the question: "What shall we work on?" The basic problem was that these professionals lacked the direction and constraints that would ordinarily have been provided by their organization through their manager. His role should be to help channel diffuse efforts toward goals that are important to the success of the organization. Many professionals want to do work that is recognized as important to the organization, since they generally see their own success as determined by their contributions to organizational goals. A management style that is permissive to the extent that it allows professionals total freedom clearly contributes to the creation of a climate of underutilization. When professionals say they want more freedom, they do not mean total freedom; they mean more influence over decisions that affect their work.

Using a participatory style of management has been widely advocated as the best way to motivate professionals, since it provides them with a considerable amount of influence in decision making about their work. In order for that approach to be effective, however, the manager should actively challenge his subordinates by giving them meaningful direction and feedback about their work. He should essentially be an integrator of ideas and information as well as a facilitator of communication. Although giving professionals freedom to explore new ideas and to pursue their own interests is quite strongly related to their being up to date, providing them with such freedom is most effective when their supervisor consults them before he makes important decisions affecting group activity.

However, provision of freedom by a supervisor may be indicative of his own lack of competence. The development of subordinates can be stimulated or stifled depending on the degree to which the supervisor has a good understanding of the knowledge and skills relevant to his work group. For example, supervisors who possess such competence can effectively stimulate their subordinates to be innovative by evaluating them critically. But critical evaluations discourage innovations if the supervisor does not have a good understanding of the knowledge and skills used by his subordinates. It is the recognized competence of the manager, rather than his human relations skills, that is most important in encouraging professionals to keep up to date. Respect for their supervisor's competence and judgment is the most important reason professionals comply with his directives. That expertise is the most prominent basis for supervisory influence and it also has a very strong relationship to the knowledge, contributions, satisfaction, and performance of subordinates.

To provide professionals with a challenging work climate, the manager himself must be relatively up to date in knowledge and skills relevant to his work group. The managers of professional groups generally have dual roles that involve specialist and management expertise. In most professional work groups, the supervisor does not necessarily have to be the most competent in the specialty, but he must possess the management expertise that is the basis of his influence in the group. That is true even among technical supervisors, as is attested to by a project manager's comment:

> There's no question about the fact that most of them (project team members) are better technically than I am. I do have the edge on them in terms of knowing about the management responsibilities associated with my project. I'm the one responsible for the project's management control systems. I'm the one who knows whether this input or that change will affect our cost and schedule objectives. I have to be on top of these

details. They have to rely on me to handle these management decisions; none of them have had any business management experience.[5]

Not only does the expertise of supervisors affect the behavior of professional subordinates but the competence of executives can contribute to the performance of the managers who work for them. Many writers have emphasized the need for managers to have upward influence, but it may be even more important for them to be recognized as competent by their subordinates as well as by their supervisors. In fact, influence in organizational decision making is determined, to a large degree, by whether or not managers possess expertise relevant to the types of decisions being made. Having expert information *is* influence.

A climate that discourages obsolescence can be created by the more competent manager, who will not be afraid of using new methods. For example, professionals whose managers encourage them to use major technical advances tend to be more up to date in their specialties. On the other hand, professionals whose managers emphasize meeting schedules tend to be more obsolescent. Since the manager may determine how the work of his group is distributed, he can use the work itself to motivate his subordinates to stay up to date. For instance, the manager can require his subordinates to become competent in several areas to avoid obsolescence, as in the following case of a supervisor dealing with a professional who had become too specialized and was resistant to change:

> I have been trying to get him to enlarge his area of competence since he has a reputation for being a specialist in a certain area which creates problems at the termination of a project. As a result of this, I have undertaken to force him into competence in other areas. My first experiment with him has been quite successful; although he has moaned and groaned, he has exhibited a good ability to perform the other jobs that I have given him. . . . I think his problem was a fear of failure. Having never done it before, I think he was more concerned with whether he was going to fall flat on his face. . . . The basic

characteristics of the individual as such are that any assignment that I would give him would probably be within his capabilities. I think as a result of his first straying from his area of specialty, he will be more willing now to enter new assignments.

Just as managers can stimulate their subordinates to stay up to date through challenging and diverse work assignments, so too they may contribute to obsolescence by assigning work that does not properly utilize professional knowledge and skills. The following example describes a specialist's complaints about how his supervisor assigns work:

Too often I have the feeling that my talents and those of other [specialists] are not being fully utilized. Presently management (first line) seems more interested in assigning a project number to a [specialist] than in actually assigning him a work task. Once the project number has been assigned the manager feels his responsibility has been fulfilled, even though actual work on the project may not be scheduled to begin for months. This is not merely my opinion, but has also been expressed by other [specialists].[6]

The two preceding cases contrast the *innovative* supervisor who attempts to motivate his subordinates through the work itself with the *inactive* supervisor who is passive and permissive and lacks initiative in stimulating the development of his subordinates. It should be rather clear then, that the manager's style, combined with his expertise, can be a powerful influence in creating a climate of utilization and challenge that can motivate professionals to keep up to date. Since the manager can have a direct influence on the updating behavior of his subordinates, more will be said of his role in promoting continuing education in the next chapter.

Management Policies

Although the individual manager can strongly affect whether or not his subordinates stay up to date, even he is limited by external constraints in the organizational climate created by higher management policies. For example, policies concerned with schedules can foster an atmosphere of misutilization, as one angry engineer describes:

> Engineering is required to do too many mundane, trivial details. At times, I feel like an IBM printer pushing out paper work. Is this really necessary? Why pay someone an engineer's salary to do something a robot could do? All in all I would say that my attitude toward [the company] would improve 100 percent if top-level management (the boys who decide schedules) realized that people are not machines and can't be worked 24 hours a day 7 days a week.[7]

If management policy creates a climate of misutilization, it practically guarantees obsolescence among professionals in the organization. Witness the following comments by a professional:

> This is a sore point with me and my blood boils when I read in the journals about obsolescence. If you run into obsolescence in a company like this, I feel quite sure that the company has an awful big hand in it. If you spend your time doing routine jobs in a company, then I think you have a great probability of becoming obsolete. If I am obsolete, this is the reason why. I've had to spend hours and days and weeks of time doing routine things.[8]

Complaints like the preceding one are quite common. In one study of defense industries it was found that 60 percent of the professionals felt that their training was not utilized. When asked to state the reasons why it was not utilized, the chief reason given was that management policies *discouraged* full utilization. The reasons are listed in Table 4, and on examination it becomes obvious that practically all of them had to do with the way the work was assigned. The assignment was determined not only by the immediate supervisor but by management policies as well. That is not as surprising as it may seem if we consider that the professionals were employed in defense industries, where professional "bodies" were frequently allocated to projects in anticipation of rather than because of the actual existence of work assignments. In fact, according to one defense systems analyst: "the overelaborated systems approach to management encourages overstaffing at every level. This generates a great deal of . . . ennui born of too little constructive work." [9] Although underutilization can be an intended result of management policy decisions, it more frequently occurs as an unintended consequence of organizational climate related to policy. Let us now see how such policies affect organizational communication, influence, uncertainty, and rewards.

COMMUNICATION, INFLUENCE, AND UNCERTAINTY

The importance of communication to the obsolescence of professionals was emphasized in the discussion about the effects

TABLE 4   Reasons for underutilization (sample size = 511).

REASONS	PERCENTAGE OF UNDERUTILIZATION
Management policies discouraged full utilization.	22.4
Was engaged in work different from what was trained for.	21.7
Unchallenging and unstimulating work.	13.1
Company needed a person with less education and training.	12.7
Too much administrative work—too many meetings.	9.5
Company did not need a technically trained person.	8.4
Job required skills in too narrow a specialization.	5.2
Others.	7.0
Total	100.0

SOURCE: R. P. Loomba, *An Examination of the Engineering Profession* (San Jose, Calif.: Center for Interdisciplinary Studies, San Jose State College, 1968), p. 80.

of colleague interaction. To a large extent, management policies determine the communications climate in the organization.[10] However, one of the major complaints of professionals at all levels of the organizational hierarchy is the lack of regular information exchange among departments as well as between different levels in the organizational hierarchy. Yet open communication channels can go a long way toward creating an organizational atmosphere that stimulates professional learning, as exhibited by the following observation by professionals: "Communication is very open here—the company is wonderful in this way. The whole atmosphere facilitates professional growth and is responsive to my needs." [11]

A climate of open communication also is a prerequisite if professionals are to influence decisions in the organization. However, professionals are frequently denied the opportunity to influence any company policies owing to a communications structure that insulates them from important decision-making processes. As one professional union representative explained:

> In recent years our members have learned the bitter truth that attempts to influence the employer's policies in *any* area constitute an almost impossible task. The principal reason is that, in the field of industrial employment of professionals, there are more levels of supervisory and managerial authority than in any other segment of industrial employment. The lines of communication between the salaried professional and the management level at which effective influence can be exerted on the employer's policy are so long, so inefficient, and so fluid as to be useless.[12]

Management policies that create a climate in which professionals have little or no influence on decisions that affect their work tend to result in widespread underutilization. A lack of influence is also related to the degree of uncertainty in the work environment. Although uncertainty can be affected by the technology of the organization as well as the function of the group (for example, research and marketing have a greater uncertainty than production and sales), management policies appear to play an important role as well. Professionals in organizations in which management policies create a climate of uncertainty have been found to experience problems of influence and of underutilization as well. Such a climate may involve frequent changes or cancellations in scheduled objectives, job requirements that are not clear, misinformation, and work about which the organization does not provide adequate or frequent enough feedback.

Not surprisingly, obsolescence increases when professionals are uncertain about the future of their work. In such a climate, they are less likely to take risks. They therefore avoid the uncertain frontiers of knowledge and instead stay with the known techniques to help create a sense of certainty in their work environment. Hence, policies, or lack of policies, that create an organizational climate fraught with uncertainty have pervasive effects on the individual and the organization. The symptoms are poor communication, limited influence, and underutilization among professionals—all of which can contribute to obsolescence. However, the most important policies directly affecting obsolescence are those that determine whether or not professional growth and development are rewarded by the organization. We will now turn to this crucial issue.

REWARD CLIMATE

There is evidence that the reward climate created by management policies can go far toward enhancing or inhibiting obsolescence.[13] If professionals see that their efforts in self-development are not rewarded by the organization, the likelihood that they will become obsolescent is increased. For example, in one study of government professionals, over 80 percent wanted their organization to stress the importance of having up-to-date knowledge in their fields, but only about one-third expected that gaining that knowledge would have an increased effect on future salary increases and promotions.

The effects of reward climate appear to be profound, since those professionals become obsolescent who feel that keeping themselves abreast of new developments will not result in more challenging work assignments or salary increases and promotions. On the other hand, those who perceive that their organizations reward updating with challenging work, promotions, and pay are also the most up to date. In a study of computer marketing and support professionals, participation in self-development activities was perceived as most likely to lead to worthwhile accomplishment and self-esteem as well as opportunities for promotion to a better job. Furthermore, the perceived expectations that organizational rewards would be forthcoming for updating efforts were significantly associated with current and future efforts at self-development. The evidence is very clear that the reward climate of the organization is intimately related to the effort expended by professionals to stay up to date.

However, even if organizations *do* reward professional development, the older professional may be excluded. For example, there is evidence that for older managers, those who possess the *most* initiative, self-assurance, and intelligence, tend to be rewarded the *least,* although the opposite is true for younger managers. Perhaps this is in line with the assumption that older professionals are more obsolescent and the organization should not waste its financial resources on their development. By discouraging the development of the older professionals who are most capable of and still desire growth, management avoids having to make an investment that it believes is likely to provide a short-lived and limited rate of return to the organization. Such a management policy creates a climate in the organization that tends to reinforce the self-fulfilling prophecy that obsolescence is inevitable with increasing age. However, rewarding self-development reinforces motivation toward professional growth even among older individuals, who, because of their experiences and loyalty, can contribute greatly to their organization if they are encouraged to remain up to date.

THE DUAL LADDER: A DUBIOUS REWARD SYSTEM

Some organizations have attempted to deal with the problem of rewarding professionals by establishing a dual ladder of advancement.[14] The dual-ladder approach is generally formalized into parallel hierarchies; one provides a managerial career path, and the other advancement as a professional or staff member. Ostensibly, the dual ladder promises equal status and rewards to equivalent levels in both hierarchies. This should provide cosmopolitan or professionally oriented individuals an opportunity and incentive to remain in their fields and thereby stay up to date by continuing to utilize their knowledge and skills without the distraction of administrative work.

Although the dual-ladder approach sounds quite feasible, there are some flaws in its logic and application that have made it unworkable in practice. First of all, the assumption that organizational professionals are cosmopolitan in their orientation is generally not true. In fact, it is only among scientists that a cosmopolitan orientation exists to any great degree; engineers, business professionals, and computer specialists are generally local (that is, organizational) in their orientation. Since the managerial ladder provides for the fulfillment of local goals (for example, promotion), it should be desired over the staff hierarchy by most organizational professionals. It has been pointed out that the professional ladder was superimposed on an existing reward system that provided promotion to greater authority rather than to greater autonomy. By removing a professional from the organizational mainstream, the professional hierarchy "gives freedom in place of power, but power is needed to remain free. Moreover . . . appointment to a [professional] ladder position is . . . a judgment that the incumbent is unfit to exercise power."[15]

The above analysis is that of an organizational researcher, but professionals themselves tend to support it. One manager who was asked why he preferred the managerial ladder answered: "Power! To be brutally frank, power! You see, in this position I have some say in policy decisions."[16] Interestingly enough, on entering an organization professionals first tend to view the staff hierarchy as equivalent to, or more attractive than, the managerial one. However, once they get on the professional ladder, they realize that the managerial side is more attractive and would provide them with more chance to make important technical decisions.

Once in the organization, professionals accept the norms and symbols of success as determined by organizational policies. Hence it should be obvious that there is an inherent weakness in the dual-ladder approach. If the ladder works the way it is intended to work, it will remove the most professionally competent people from positions of influence in the organization. Indeed, it has been observed that productivity falls off after individuals are appointed to positions on the professional ladder. That is not surprising, since their removal from the organizational mainstream means they have essentially been identified as inadequate to exercise leadership skills.

However, there is evidence that the dual ladder does in fact reward those who are most professionally competent and up to date, but by advancement in the managerial and not the professional hierarchy. Therefore, the reward system itself may ultimately contribute to obsolescence, since competent professionals are rewarded by promotions into management and eventually they may have to divert time and energy away from keeping abreast of new developments. It is possible for organizations to create a climate that is both rewarding and stimulating to self-development, but that may require a major commitment to organizational change and development, to which we shall now turn.

Organizational Change and Development

For any type of organizational change and development to be carried out successfully, it is imperative that top management be totally committed to all aspects of the change program; it must desire the change.[17] Unfortunately, this is the greatest stumbling block to creating a climate that encourages utilization and self-development. Even programs of job design and enrichment must involve changes in organizational policy that are under executive control. This is attested to by an up-to-date manager working in a changing environment who responded to the question of how he might redesign his job to make it better for him personally:

> That's a very tough one to answer because it would involve changing completely the policies under which we operate. . . .
>
> I have a personal opinion that the way we operate could be improved by many changes . . . but you have to educate top management on what you're trying to do. . . .
>
> Now, we *do* change. We have a great deal of authority in our operations here. We can make a great many changes. Only when we get into policy problems do we have to go to our management.[18]

It is rather evident from the preceding example that even when there is a great deal of authority to carry out change at the operating level, policy made at the highest organizational levels can prevent change from occurring. In most organizations it would probably be necessary to modify the entire management system from the top down before the lowest levels could have the real responsibility that techniques such as job enrichment are intended to provide. The control system must be modified to allow professionals increased responsibility for decision making, particularly with regard to resource allocation, work assignments, and time schedules. Broad and reasonable constraints can be provided by higher-level management, but ultimate responsibility should rest with the professionals and their supervisors. If higher management is committed to such change efforts, then commitment from lower-level management should be forthcoming.

To create an organization with a flexible control system, not only must all levels of management cooperate in dealing with change but the professionals themselves must be included in any problem-solving team whose function is to redesign their own jobs as well as the organizational control system. Professionals will readily accept a true participative and active role in restructuring the organization and their jobs, especially when it is relevant to shaping their own careers. Such an approach, if it is carried out on a regular basis, can go far to increase influence, improve communication, reduce uncertainties, and properly utilize the knowledge and skills of professional employees.

There is clear evidence that providing professionals with increased policy-making authority can create a reward system that reinforces competence in their specialties. Perhaps a relevant illustration is the change carried out by a small company in merging its dual-ladder reward system into a single management hierarchy. Professionals were assigned to relatively lower positions on the merged ladder than they had on the staff ladder. Did they feel a diminished status or fear that the utilization of their expertise was being threatened? To the contrary, as the following description notes:

> Even though they got lower formal positions, they were evidently pleased to be where it was possible to have power. Fifty-four per cent of them said that their goals were better served by the change, and only 15 per cent felt that they had lost ground. They now attended policy-making management meetings and shared authority and status with those in supervisory management. . . .
>
> The relevance of power to even the technically oriented engineer is shown by the very favorable responses to the new arrangement by those . . . who were most concerned with technical expertise. . . .
>
> [The data] indicate that the more importance one accorded to being a technical authority and the higher one rates himself in technical ability, the more he thought his goals were better served by the change away from a professional-ladder structure.[19]

The new organizational structure was now serving to satisfy the goals of the professionals for whom staying competent in their fields was extremely important. Apparently the new reward system provided the most competent with the greatest influence in policy making. It is possible that the old system was rewarding incompetence.

ORGANIZATIONAL STRUCTURE

Flat vs. tall structures. The way the organization is structured has a profound effect on the growth and development of its professionals. For example, an important dimension of organizational structure is the number of levels in the management hierarchy. Attaining success in so-called flat organizations, in which there are few levels of management control, contributes to satisfying the growth needs of professionals. However, in tall organizations, in which there are many levels of management control, the attainment of success bears no relation to how well growth needs are satisfied.[20] Furthermore, those who are most competent are more likely to rise to higher-level positions in flat than in tall organizations. It appears that not only do professionals have greater opportunities to exhibit individual responsibility, initiative, and self-expression in flat organizations but the structure more readily permits the encouragement and rewarding of such behavior. Thus, reducing the number of levels in the management hierarchy would be a relatively simple way to increase the flexibility of the control system and encourage professional growth and development.

Function vs. product. To enhance growth, organizations may have to make changes that require more complex restructuring than merely reducing the number of management levels. How are professionals best organized so that they, as well as the organization, do not become obsolescent? A dilemma with which management has long grappled is whether to organize professionals into groups according to (1) their common functional specialty such as engineering or marketing or (2) a common product or project that utilizes specialists across disciplines.[21] Of the two approaches, the functional organization permits the maximum utilization of professional knowledge and skills on different projects or products and consequently stimulates its members to stay up to date.

However, one of the major management problems in functional organizations is to integrate and coordinate the various specialties in order to be able to respond to rapid changes in the market with new products completed on schedule and within budgetary constraints. To facilitate integration, coordination, and communication among functional groups working on different products, many organizations have adopted compromise solutions that involve changing the control structure. Perhaps the most complex of such integrative changes combines the functional and product forms by overlaying them into what has come to be known as a matrix organization.

Matrix organization. Typically, the matrix approach preserves the functional specialist groups, but the groups share authority with product management and the result is a dual integrated authority system. The authority can be concentrated either in functional or in product management. The appropriate concentration of control is determined by such factors as the diversity of product line, the rate of change in productivity, interdependence among specialties, tightness of schedules, and size of the organization. However, the more crucial expertise is to the organization's competitive effectiveness and ultimate survival, the more influence should be provided to functional management. The matrix approach can overcome problems of communication, influence in decision making, and uncertainty relevant to meeting product goals while it utilizes and develops the knowledge and skills of functional specialists.

From the examples of structural change we have looked at, it is clear that if organizations want to pay more than mere lip service to professional development and growth, they must carefully examine the effects of their policies and control systems on individual competence and organizational effectiveness. By restructuring the influence and reward systems so that they stimulate professional competence while simultaneously attaining organizational goals, management can come close to bringing obsolescence under control.

WE HAVE SEEN that the organizational climate can stimulate or stifle professional development and growth. Three aspects of organizational climate have been discussed: (1) colleague interaction and communication, (2) leadership style and expertise, and (3) management policies. These dimensions of climate are crucial in determining organizational communication, influence, uncertainty, and the reward structure, all of which affect professional utilization and obsolescence. Since these climate factors can to a large degree be controlled by management, the work environment can be transformed, by organizational change and development, into one that stimulates and nurtures professional growth. The following are among the approaches that have been suggested for creating a climate that can stifle obsolescence.

1. Organize work groups to include specialists with a diversity of backgrounds and change the composition of these groups periodically to assure a steady stimulation to learn new knowledge and skills.

2. Include in each work group a gatekeeper who will provide the professionals with relevant information from within and outside the organization.

3. When a specialist with new skills is brought into an existing work group, the other professionals in the group should learn these new skills as well.

4. Select managers of professionals on the basis of their competence and expertise in the knowledge and skills possessed by their work group.

5. Managers should help integrate relevant ideas and information as well as facilitate communication for their work group by consulting their subordinates about important decisions and providing them with feedback and meaningful direction about their work.

6. Managers should be *innovative* in providing their subordinates with active stimulation and encouragement to acquire new knowledge and skills.

7. Management policies should be so formulated that they require professionals to utilize their knowledge and skills in appropriate work assignments.

8. Management policy should explicitly encourage and reward professional growth and development throughout the

career by assigning more challenging and responsible work, as well as by providing salary increases and promotions to those who maintain their competence by keeping up to date.

9. Involve professionals in changing the organizational structure to attain a more flexible control system that will reduce uncertainty as well as increase communication and influence at the lowest levels of the hierarchy.

10. Organize professionals by function in a matrix organization if necessary, and reduce the levels in the management hierarchy in order to create a climate that stimulates professional competence and influence.

Such changes as these will create a climate in which job design and enrichment, as well as the other personnel techniques described in earlier chapters, can be effectively applied to bring obsolescence under control. However, all these approaches are indirect, albeit quite effective, strategies for attacking obsolescence, and it would be appropriate to complete our discussion by focusing on the more direct methods having to do with continuing education, which is the subject of the next chapter.

Chapter 7

Continuing Education: Panacea or Palliative?

SINCE THE PROBLEM of obsolescence has been attributed by most authorities to the explosive growth rate of new knowledge, organizations have responded with what they believe to be an appropriate remedy: continuing education. Indicative of such an analysis is the exhortation by a partner of Price Waterhouse & Company:

> As viewed from the world of business, what was studied in college is yesterday's knowledge. But what will be needed for a future business career is tomorrow's knowledge . . . no matter how much education one has, it is not enough. It will not last a lifetime; it will soon be obsolete. Unless one devotes time and energy to continue his education, he will become an educational dropout. Don't let it happen to you! [1]

Given the prevalence of such attitudes in business and industry, it is easy to understand why the mushrooming of organizational support for professional training and education activities has paralleled the knowledge explosion. For example, a 1962 survey of companies indicated that the increase of expenditures for professional education activities ranged from three to eight times the amount spent ten years previously for this purpose.[2] By the mid-1960s allocations by business and industry for educational activities were estimated at an astounding $17 billion. Major corporations have built multi-million dollar campuses for their employees, and some even offer degrees from their own schools. Indeed, it is rare today for an organization not to provide support for some type of continuing-education program for its professionals. In this chapter we will closely examine the continuing-education activities of organizational professionals to determine the degree to which they contribute to updating, and how the effectiveness of such activities can be improved.

Do Professionals Participate in Continuing Education?

How have professionals responded to the proliferation of opportunities for continuing education offered them by their organizations? [3] To begin with, a survey of 4,400 technical professionals has revealed that the most important objectives in taking courses would be to keep from becoming obsolete and to prepare for increased responsibility, as can be seen from Table 5. Although two-thirds see continuing education

TABLE 5   Importance of objectives in getting additional education or training among 4,400 technical professionals.

OBJECTIVE	PERCENT SAYING OF UTMOST IMPORTANCE
To keep from becoming obsolete.	64.3
To prepare myself for increased responsibility.	62.8
To perform my present assignment better.	44.8
To remedy deficiencies in my initial training.	38.8
To obtain an advanced degree.	34.2
To enable me to become an authority in my field of specialty.	34.1
Because my manager expects his people to take additional course work.	6.6

as important for staying up to date and for their career development, fewer than half feel that they would take courses to improve their present job performance or to remedy deficiencies in their initial training. Interestingly enough, only one out of three would participate in continuing education to obtain an advanced degree or to become an authority in the field.

Since professionals view education and training as important to their future careers and staying up to date, it would be expected that their rate of participation in continuing education would be quite high. However, the evidence is to the contrary, despite the fact that their organizations offer a generous potpourri of continuing-education opportunities. For example, a nationwide survey carried out during the mid-1960s revealed that almost half of all engineers had never participated in any noncredit education or training and over two-thirds had not attended graduate school. In addition, many of the courses taken by engineers are not technical in nature but are management-oriented. If technical professionals, who generally are the people most affected by obsolescence, are not taking courses to stay up to date in their fields, participation in continuing education among other organizational professionals is in all likelihood even more limited.

The reasons most frequently cited by professionals for not taking courses involve a lack of time because of other obligations, usually to family and job. As we shall see, however, many organizations do not provide a climate that would encourage their professionals to make an effort to continue their education, even if they were self-motivated. This appears to be contradictory to organizational policies of providing education and training opportunities especially for the purpose of controlling obsolescence. Indeed, the evidence is rather clear that although higher management may believe it is encouraging and even rewarding self-development activities, formal policies are not being communicated to the working-level professionals in practice. An excellent example is the discrepancy in responses between personnel representatives and engineers with regard to whether their organizations have a policy of encouraging and rewarding continuing-education activities. This is detailed in the first two rows of Table 6.

To judge by the evidence in Table 6, not only do over half of the organizations *not* encourage or reward continuing-education activities, but even when they say they do, the professionals tend not to agree that such is the case. Although there may be a formal top-level policy encouraging continuing education, the problem appears to be one of implementation at the working level by the manager of the professional work group, as the following observation by one such manager indicates:

> I think there's more than one manager who has said that: "Don't bother taking a course in that. You can pick whatever

TABLE 6   Personnel representatives' and engineers' views on activities encouraged and rewarded by organizations.

ACTIVITY	"ENCOURAGES MUCH"		"REWARDS MUCH"	
	PER- SONNEL	ENGI- NEERS	PER- SONNEL	ENGI- NEERS
Advanced degree work	42%	23%	44%	24%
Refresher courses	41	20	25	12
Belonging to professional societies	39	20	12	5
Papers at professional engineering meetings	36	15	10	6
Attendance at professional engineering meetings	35	16	19	4
Becoming a registered professional engineer	31	17	14	7
Publication in professional engineering journals	27	14	11	7
Pursuing "pet" projects on company time	2	1	2	1

SOURCE: R. Perrucci and J. E. Gerstl, *Profession Without Community: Engineers in American Society* (New York: Random House, 1969), p. 122.

you need to know up much more easily." And these are people who are too smart to discourage your interest in broadening yourself. But the implication is clear that it won't make any difference in your next raise or promotion if you take that course or not. The Laboratory Manager might be shocked at that.

The crucial link between organizational policy on updating and its operational implementation is the immediate supervisor. As can be seen from Table 5, very few professionals would take courses because their managers expect them to. In fact, all studies seem to be unanimous in their findings that there is a strong tendency for professionals to feel that their supervisors were noncommittal or did not encourage education or training even when it was job-directed. As one Ph.D. physicist noted about his responses to the questions concerning his supervisor's attitude toward continuing education: "I have circled 'noncommittal' although 'discourages me' might be a better choice. Despite his obvious distaste for losing my productive capacity to attend courses, I have been able to go." [4]

Other responses were similar: the supervisors did not want to lose the valuable productive time of their professionals who would be away from the job involved in a continuing-education activity. Such supervisors tend to work in organizational climates that focus on accomplishing the immediate tasks, and they consequently tend to discourage activities that reduce productive work time. Climates that neither encourage nor reward professional updating have been found to be prevalent in the construction, chemical, and petroleum industries and in local governments. On the other hand, there are supervisors who work in organizational climates that actively encourage and even reward continuing-education efforts. Such climates have been found most frequently in organizations where new developments and change are part of the work environment, such as those in R&D, aerospace, and the federal government. However, it has been found that, even in situations where continuing education is rewarded, taking more than two courses per term may be discouraged by the supervisor because it can interfere with immediate job requirements.

It does seem rather curious that there should be such a limited use and encouragement of continuing-education programs, if organizations and professionals alike are concerned about obsolescence and courses are provided to combat it. We have already seen that course taking may be discouraged because it could interfere with immediate productivity, but perhaps there may even be a question whether the knowledge gained from formal courses for updating can offset lost productive working time. Are organizations being short-sighted in emphasizing goals of immediate productivity? Do formal courses help increase the value and useful life of professional manpower and thereby contribute to the maintenance of the organization? Although these questions cannot be answered unequivocally, there is some evidence that certain course modes are more effective than others.

Effects of Formal Courses on Obsolescence

Although many course modes for professional updating are available, the majority of offerings are either university-sponsored graduate-level courses or formal in-house training programs. There are great differences in the two modes, not only in their objectives and content but also in their effectiveness in dealing with obsolescence of professionals.

GRADUATE-LEVEL COURSES

Graduate-level courses are typically offered by colleges or universities to degree-seeking students, but they may also be taken on a nondegree or even noncredit basis.[5] Some university-sponsored courses are designed to help professionals stay abreast of the latest developments in their field, and are generally not offered for formal credit. Most organizations provide partial or full reimbursement for university-sponsored courses taken on a part-time basis (generally two courses per semester), and many also provide released time from work to attend class. A significant number of organizations provide leaves to do full-time resident graduate work. Most frequently the leaves are without pay, but some organizations do provide for partial or even full pay while the professional is engaged in study. Regardless of the type of incentive provided, most organizations require that the courses be work-related to qualify for support. In addition, organizations generally require that grades be submitted if students are to receive tuition refunds. Some organizations even have a graduated reward system: the higher the grade, the greater the percent of tuition that is refunded.

Given that the half-life of a professional education may be as short as five years in some fields, it would appear that some continuing education is necessary to keep the professional from becoming obsolete. Indeed, there is consistent evidence that professionals who have taken graduate courses are perceived as less obsolescent by themselves, their supervisors, and their colleagues. Furthermore, taking a large number of graduate courses is not seen as any different from obtaining a master's degree for keeping professionals current. In fact, of those professionals who do take such courses, many are not in degree programs, which indicates that their primary motivation is to obtain knowledge by continuing their education. Most professionals feel that their colleagues who undertake graduate study do so for the useful knowledge they obtain from courses rather than for the recognition of the degree. Is participation in university-sponsored courses in reality useful for averting obsolescence? There is some evidence that it is.

The unemployment-reemployment experiences of professionals have sometimes been used as indirect measures of obsolescence. For example, a study of 125 technical professionals laid off at one time by a large division of a major corporation revealed "one interesting constant among all—not one had taken any form of extracurricular education in the past six years." [6] According to another study, the mere fact that one is enrolled in a graduate-level program is one of the major determinants of how long it takes the unemployed professional to become reemployed. The latter finding supported the following conclusion: "If enrollment in a master's or doctor's program can be regarded as an attempt to stave off obsolescence and thereby improve reemployment opportunities, it seems to be working very well." [7]

Although age has been found to be strongly associated with length of unemployment among professionals, research results have demonstrated that "as the degree level goes up, the influence of age on the period of unemployment decreases continuously. . . . It appears, therefore, that one way of combatting old age is to obtain a higher degree." [8] The same research also found that professionals report that their formal education was the single most helpful factor in obtaining a postlayoff job.

Since it has been argued that obsolescence may be only one of several factors contributing to length of unemployment and that graduate education may no longer have the same salutary effects on reemployment, it is necessary to look at other, more direct evidence of a relationship between graduate education and obsolescence. A nationwide study of 3,000 engineers found an overall pattern of graduate education inhibiting obsolescence and concluded that such education "apparently imparts both the knowledge and the motivation for maintaining knowledge necessary to minimize the degree of obsolescence." [9] A study of 2,500 technical professionals in six organizations found that not only were those with graduate training at the M.S. level better performers than those who had only a B.S. but their high performance was maintained ten years after the B.S. holders began to decline in performance. It would appear that a heavy dosage of graduate courses can push obsolescence back by ten years.

Perhaps the most convincing evidence that graduate courses can affect both job assignment and professional obsolescence is to be found in a study of 110 engineers from three organizations who were followed up during the first 14 years of their careers. One interesting result was that the number of graduate courses completed had little or no relationship to job performance or professional contributions during their early years of experience, but that when they reached mid-career, significant effects did appear. The strongest effect was on professional contributions, which became significantly higher in number for those with more graduate courses. Performance is affected by graduate education only after a decade of experience, which possibly indicates that the half-life of those who did not continue their education was beginning to take its toll.

It would appear, then, that participation in graduate courses does reinforce the breadth and depth of knowledge that is indispensable in preventing both professional and job assignment obsolescence, particularly at mid-career. The discipline and comprehensiveness of graduate-level courses help professionals diversify their in-depth knowledge about new fields actually or potentially related to their work. Such courses allow them to acquire the fundamentals of a subject so they can continue learning about new developments in their area by self-instruction. However, since few curricula are at the frontiers of knowledge, graduate-level courses serve primarily to provide the basis for professional updating by self-development, as is indicated in a comment by one professional:

> I don't think taking course work in a university is a means of keeping yourself up to date. There aren't too many schools teaching courses at the frontiers. Most courses are background and basic. A few are taught from the literature and they are current. There are advanced courses but they're classic, not on the edge of current work. But there are some which are based on the ideas of the past two or three years. These are a small proportion of the curriculum. In general, courses are to bring you to the point where you can pioneer new areas.[10]

There are some graduate-level courses that deal with the frontiers of knowledge, such as the noncredit "State of the Arts" program at Northeastern University. The teachers in this program are themselves practitioners who are key contributors to new developments in their field. However, the usefulness of university courses for updating professionals may be limited, since those people who have the greatest predisposition to become obsolescent are not the ones who participate in graduate courses. It is primarily the younger professionals who enroll in graduate-level courses, and not those who have been out of school for many years. Older professionals are frequently very reluctant and even afraid to take courses that are demanding or that require prerequisites which the individual out of school for many years is not likely to have. Such fears were expressed by a 50-year-old with an M.S. in response to a question about why he had not taken any additional graduate courses:

> I think some hesitation about being in a class with really young people. It's a funny atmosphere to be back in school with kids twenty years younger. There may be some conscious and unconscious hesitation. You may be competent in some area, but in a particular subject they may have just had some prerequisite course in detail. It can be an embarrassing situation, particularly in a tough school.[11]

Such hesitation is, however, apparent even among younger professionals, since it is those who have the weakest knowledge in their field to begin with, and are consequently most obsolescence-prone, who tend not to participate in graduate-level courses. Therefore, it would appear that graduate courses are effective in fighting obsolescence, but primarily among professionals who have the ability and motivation to stay up to date in their field. Those who lack these qualities are likely to avoid university-sponsored courses, but do they attempt to deal with obsolescence by other means? One possible means is by taking in-house courses in their organization.

IN-HOUSE COURSES

Many organizations offer in-house noncredit courses for their professionals on a regular basis.[12] The courses are offered primarily to supplement university-sponsored courses. They are usually more directly applicable to the work of the organization and are less demanding than are graduate courses, since they typically do not involve grades, examinations, or even homework. In-house courses are especially appealing to older professionals, who feel more comfortable and less threatened when they are learning material relevant to their jobs in a relatively noncompetitive manner. It might be expected that such courses would be ideal for helping the older professionals keep up to date, particularly with the knowledge and skills relevant to their work. However, the evidence is to the contrary. Older obsolescent professionals do take in-house courses, but the courses do not seem to help. The following case illustrates the point:

> In one company, we found that the engineers over 40 who needed and were taking company-sponsored courses were the very ones whose performance ratings declined from year to year. The managers in this company suggested that when a man's rating began to decline, he would query his supervisor and often be told that his skills were becoming obsolete and that he needed some refresher courses. But it was then too late for a few courses to arrest the decline in his performance rating.[13]

It may indeed be too late to use in-house courses to reduce obsolescence among older professionals. However, what about younger professionals, those who have just begun their careers? There is evidence that those who take in-house courses, like those who take university-level courses, tend to be relatively young, but that is as far as the similarity goes. The young in-house course takers tend to have received few promotions and to have made only modest contributions to their organizations and professions as compared with those who take university courses. Furthermore, it has been found that the more in-house courses young professionals take, the less likely they are to have enrolled in graduate courses, and the less professional knowledge they possess.

But even more revealing is the fact that professionals who were the poorest performers early in their careers tended to take the most in-house courses after they reached their half-life period (that is, between 9 and 11 years of work experience). Furthermore, those whose professional contributions were poorest after they reached their half-life tended to take more in-house courses in their subsequent careers. If such course taking is an attempt to reduce obsolescence and improve performance, its effectiveness may be limited, since enrolling in a large number of in-house courses was found to be unrelated to subsequent performance.

One explanation for the phenomenon described above comes from a finding that "some company-supported degree programs create anxiety in those who are not seeking advanced degrees." [14] It is likely that the less capable professionals who do not go on to graduate school, but who perceive that they are not keeping up to date, attempt to reduce their anxiety by participating in the less demanding in-house courses. Those whose anxiety is increased by their poor performance or few professional contributions may take a large number of in-house courses as a response to felt needs concerning inadequacies, which existed prior to course enrollment.

The needs that motivated professionals to take in-house courses in the first place are very likely not satisfied by these courses. The undemanding nature of many in-house courses may be one of the reasons why such courses do not help to eliminate symptoms of obsolescence. It is also likely that the lack of ability or motivation which contributed to the professional's obsolescence to begin with is still there, and it may preclude active learning via any type of continuing education. This is implied by a typical comment from a scientist who has taught in-house courses:

> My opinion is that courses taught here in the laboratory fall short of the rigor found on the outside. You assign homework and no one does it. That runs through all these things. The students won't get out for a company course the way they do for one they pay for and go to. [Do they learn what they need to know?] They'll learn it if the teacher can get through their apathy or whatever it is. Their attitude seems to be "if I don't have to work for it and you can pour it in, okay." I had a 50 percent mortality in my course because of this attitude. [15]

The paradox is that many professionals feel that in-house courses have advantages over graduate courses but rank them relatively low in importance for keeping people up to date compared with other modes. That paradox is implied in the following comment by a course participant:

> In-lab courses I took were to maintain a certain level of mathematical competence and to obtain some knowledge of subjects that could be useful in my field. These courses are very convenient, being offered right at the lab. . . . One bad point about these courses is that the instructor does not push the student. Sometimes tests are not given. If tests were given and the student had to work a little harder, it is my opinion that one would get much more out of these courses.[16]

Therefore, it appears that even when professionals have the ability and motivation to update themselves through in-company courses, the courses may not be demanding enough to really challenge them to learn. In addition, there does not appear to be much planning to integrate such courses to meet the updating needs of the organizational professional. For example, in one company where approximately 20 in-house courses are offered annually, a supervisor observed:

> It's a catch as catch can proposition. There is no order in these courses. When [there is] enough clamor for a course, then it is given. If you miss it, you never know when it will be offered again. There is a need to plan them farther in advance, find out what a person would find helpful. Now a decision is made on the basis of filling up a class.[17]

The feelings of this supervisor appear to reflect a rather widespread problem with in-house courses. In fact, a survey of over 70 companies revealed that partly "because of a lack of unification of courses for nonsupervisors, anti-obsolescence effectiveness in the sponsorship of company courses appeared limited." [18]

The problem of lack of planning updating programs is not unique to in-house courses; it pertains to the whole spectrum of organization-sponsored continuing-education activities. It seems rather clear that the updating potential of in-house courses has generally not been taken advantage of, primarily because little or no management effort is directed toward planning and integrating such courses to meet individual as well as organizational needs.

Integrating Continuing Education with Individual and Organizational Goals

Indeed, very little thought has been given by most organizations to planning broad integrated continuing-education programs in general to serve the updating needs of both the individual and the organization. Graduate and in-house courses are expensive; and if they are not properly planned for the individual, they can be a waste of time and money for all concerned. The emphasis on formal education and training as the cure for obsolescence, which exists in some organizations, merely relieves management of the responsibility to analyze the problem and to develop more meaningful approaches to updating, as the following comments by two professionals would suggest:

> I'm sure there must be some technical obsolescence, but I don't think it exists the way the administration thinks it does. They start training courses during the day, but I am against that. It takes people away from their work, and I consider the best way to keep up to date is to read the technical journals rather than take courses, and I still think there are many people who could work on their own job and continue their education.[19]

> .   .   .

> The corporation places too much emphasis on education, just for the sake of exercising one's brain. It's very frustrating to spend many hours on education—at the suggestion of management—only to find in a year's time, we've forgotten what we learned.[20]

It is obvious from such statements that formal course work is not being used effectively even when it is encouraged by the organization. What, then, can organizations do to improve the effectiveness of continuing-education programs for professional updating? As a general answer, organizations must integrate educational programs with their own goals as well as those of their professionals. More specifically, they can do this in a number of ways:

Use the work itself to motivate continuing education.[21] The statements of the two professionals quoted above indicate that formal courses can be irrelevant or even detrimental to the professional's work role. The crux of the problem is whether the professional will utilize what he learns in formal courses either in his current job or later in his career, preferably at an increased level of responsibility. However, there is evidence that, for many professionals, course participation is often an escape from job stagnation, and not much benefit appears to be derived from most formal courses under those circumstances. When the work environment requires the use of up-to-date knowledge and skills, then professionals will be motivated to go out and learn. As was discussed in Chapter 5, it is the challenge of the work itself that stimulates and reinforces professional growth and development. Continuing education also can be encouraged in such a manner, as the following study found:

> In many ways on-the-job activities, when varied to include new and challenging assignments, become opportunities for self-assessment, which in turn provide a basis for additional learning and development. It appears, therefore, that if continuing education is to culminate in meaningful productive output, an on-the-job awareness of the need for improvement should be the first step in any such program.[22]

As has already been discussed in Chapter 6, the immediate supervisor plays an important role in creating a climate which encourages such self-development. The supervisor can even provide innovative stimulation for those who have lost motivation to keep up to date. For example:

> Some supervisors try to manipulate or influence the environment which surrounds the person who appears to be in need of some form of help. These supervisors often attempt to intro-

duce new and diverse work situations which will force this person to cope with problems he has not met before. The manager may deliberately introduce stress in the individual by changing his work assignment to a new but related area, or he may change the person's project altogether. These tactics are aimed at impersonally enforcing some form of continuing education which will cope with the new problems to be faced.[23]

From everything that has been said thus far, it is quite evident that continuing education is effective primarily insofar as it responds to the work-related needs of the professional. Consequently, professional jobs should be redesigned to increase the utilization of knowledge and skills, which in turn will stimulate meaningful updating activities in a continuous process of applying and reinforcing that which has been learned.

Assess the continuing-education needs of individual professionals. As is obvious from some of the complaints about continuing education, there is a crucial need to determine what courses, if any, professionals will find useful to their job and profession. Management should assess professional training and development needs in the organization as an essential step prior to allocating resources to continuing education. Such an assessment should have two objectives: (1) to provide management with a complete and accurate picture of overall professional continuing-education needs in the organization; and (2) to identify specific continuing-education needs of individual professionals.

One recently developed approach utilizes a computerized survey technique to enable organizations to rapidly and inexpensively identify the continuing-education needs of professional personnel.[24] The topics included in the survey reflect those fields or subjects which are relevant to the organization's activities and goals. The survey ultimately generates a description of the organization's overall continuing-education requirements, as well as of specific educational programs most pertinent to individual career development. This assessment program can be administered periodically, to monitor changes in the organization's continuing-education needs.

Such a needs assessment enables management to plan and organize more effective continuing-education programs for its professional personnel. It also helps organizations to more readily determine the demand for particular courses, the educational methods to be utilized, and manpower and budget requirements for the courses. In addition, the needs assessment can provide input to carry out individual counseling for self-development.

Provide counseling to guide continuing education. Organizations should provide counseling and guidance to increase the effectiveness of their continuing-education programs. There is evidence that most professionals look to their supervisors for guidance in their career development, yet as we have already seen, a significant number of supervisors do not provide encouragement for continuing education, and they frequently lack the competence to provide effective counseling. However, when skilled counseling *is* provided it can be quite effective in designing a multifaceted approach to updating, as in the following example:

> Sometimes "retraining" has been useless because it is wrongly chosen for the individual or because the selected courses are ineffectual. GE discovered that the "retraining value" of typical courses can be sharply increased and the effectiveness of course selection and execution greatly improved if the individual can get competent counseling to provide supervision, coordination, and full utilization of his time. In one cited GE case, a manager of an advanced design group requiring very elegant mathematical analyses was counseled to combine supplemental reading and exercise assignments in a textbook, to review advanced mathematics in programmed monographs, to attend a 2-week seminar and selected lectures in other programs, to view at home some special slide films, and to take several courses at a nearby college.[25]

Although such counseling should be part of the MBO approach used by the supervisor (see Chapter 4), assessment techniques and career counselors can also be effective, especially when the supervisor may not be aware of the different updating methods which are available.

Use innovative techniques to promote self-learning. Although formal courses can provide the foundation for updating, professionals must depend primarily on informal modes of continuing education to gain new knowledge and skills during their careers. Consequently, the objective of formal updating programs should be to motivate and prepare professionals for self-learning. Some educational specialists have suggested that formal courses which use classroom lecture approaches exclusively may not only have a limited effect in stimulating self-learning but may actually contribute to obsolescence. One such specialist explains that "the overuse of the lecture system has produced in our former students a profound distaste for self-study (and for graduate school) . . . [which] explains why obsolescence at 40 is not uncommon." [26] In a sense, professionals may be victims of an educational system that habituates them to being passive recipients of information: their learning is directed by course requirements, class assignments, teachers' instructions, and so on, and they are provided with very little opportunity to learn and practice self-direction.

Without having been given an opportunity to develop the confidence necessary to manage a program of self-education successfully, many professionals remain dependent on others for guidance. Although there is an increasing emphasis on independent study in higher education, it is difficult for many professionals to change the learning habits developed in their formative years beginning with kindergarten. Nevertheless, if organizations are committed to encouraging it among professional employees, self-learning can be accomplished, despite the inhibitions that may exist, by utilizing various innovative approaches. Examples of those approaches follow.[27]

1. Training by objectives (TBO) [28] is based on the premise that "all development is self-development," and it allows for training to be individualized to the particular person, position, and situation. As in MBO, the emphasis in TBO is on the

professionals establishing their own development goals (ones that are compatible with organizational goals) and directing their own activities toward those goals. The TBO approach seems especially useful for training employees for new job assignments. After the professional understands the overall as well as specific requirements of the job, which may be described in a self-development guide, he is given the responsibility of training himself. If necessary, a budget for travel expenses and facilities in which to carry out research are provided.

Communication is encouraged with whomever the employee feels he needs to be in touch with, inside or outside the organization, to achieve his learning goal. A series of questions is carefully designed to evaluate how well the individual has learned to master the requirements of his job assignment. Periodic progress-review sessions scheduled with the supervisor are used to evaluate the exercises performed and to discuss what additional training activities are necessary to accomplish the remaining training goals. Results have indicated that TBO not only greatly reduces the training period for new recruits but may be even more effective in retraining older individuals. Although the TBO approach appears to be useful for specific job assignment training, its real value may be in developing confidence and self-sufficiency so that learning will be continuous and at the professionals' own initiative during their subsequent careers.

2. New technologies for self-education can be utilized to help develop and reinforce self-learning behavior in professionals.[29] Although correspondence courses and programmed instruction have been available for many years, a variety of audiovisual approaches to self-study have become accessible only recently. The techniques are most appropriate for the organization that desires to be creative and effective in shaping the learning experiences and attitudes of its professionals. Examples of new multimedia technologies range from low-cost audio tape cartridge players and potentially low-cost videotape

cartridge units to relatively more expensive closed-circuit TV and computerized learning systems using individual terminals.

The hardware of new educational modes is readily available, but its effective use for individualized updating through self-study requires a high degree of creativity, ingenuity, and professionalism in the application of learning principles. Not only can flexible and individualized study programs be created to motivate active updating of professionals in particular subjects but new technology can be applied to stimulate thinking about defining new problems, experimenting with possible approaches, developing solutions, and evaluating their outcomes. Such inquiry-based learning systems typically utilize computer simulation and game techniques that allow professionals to learn how to rely on their own capabilities to deal with realistic problems—a skill grossly neglected in the education of most professionals.

However, just as providing continuing education only through classroom lectures can be relatively ineffective in promoting continuous updating, so exclusive reliance on self-study modes may not be the best approach either. Stimulation and guidance from an experienced teacher, as well as interactions with colleagues in the classroom, can contribute much to learning. There is evidence that the most effective method of continuing education combines self-study with lectures. That approach can range from independent study integrated with short intensive seminars to self-contained videotaped lectures combined with a study guide and reading assignments. Regardless of the approach, professionals are practically unanimous in feeling that the lecture part of the program provided stimulation that self-study alone would not have given. Therefore, organizations planning to utilize new educational technologies to promote self-learning would be well advised to integrate some type of human interaction mode with the audiovisual hardware to attain maximum effectiveness as well as efficiency.

3. Provision of time for self-learning. As was discussed earlier, for most professionals one of the major blocks to keep-

ing up to date is a lack of time. If organizations are serious about wanting their professionals to remain up to date, they should formalize a policy requiring some time to be set aside during working hours for self-learning.[30] The reluctance of some organizations to allow their professionals time for self-development may be based on the assumption that the time will not be used productively. To judge by the willingness of most professionals to commit time and energy to self-development, especially when it is work-related, the assumption of nonproductive time utilization is patently false. Commitment to use their time productively is demonstrated by professionals who, when asked what they would do with extra time, frequently responded that they would read, study, or work at their jobs as opposed to participating in leisure or family-oriented activities. If professionals understand that their organizations expect them to not only develop updating programs but also spend some of their time during work hours at self-study, taking formal courses, reading, and so on, they will readily acquire a strong desire for learning. Many organizations do provide released time during work hours for their professionals either to attend courses, utilize self-learning programs, or just read the current literature.

A goodly number of organizations permit their professionals to be away from their work from several days to several weeks per year to attend professional meetings or short courses relevant to their fields. Such outside activities can be quite stimulating to professional development, since they relieve the individual from work pressures and responsibility to concentrate on acquiring new knowledge. However, the time off should be provided on a selective basis because only some professionals will be able to gain significant knowledge from particular courses or meetings. Frequently, the professionals selected will be the informational gatekeepers (see Chapter 6), the key men who interface with the external world to provide new knowledge input to the organization.

A relatively small number of organizations provide time off

for sabbaticals to allow a select few of their professionals to pursue full-time study for several months or even years. Organizations should consider expanding the availability of sabbaticals to more than just a select few, because intensive full-time study may be the most effective method of extending the useful life of professionals. Indeed, opportunities for full-time study can be both a reward that professionals in their mid-career can look forward to and an important incentive to attain commitment to the organization. As one professional puts it, "The company has spent a lot of money educating me, and that makes me want to justify their faith in me." [31] In fact, there is evidence that professionals who are supported in reduced-time and educational leave programs have longer subsequent service to their organizations. In general, providing time off for self-development tends to reduce turnover and increase commitment to the organization, not to mention possible improvements in performance and professional contributions.

Improve the management of information dissemination. Since so much of the knowledge necessary for professionals to keep up to date is accessible in published form, organizations would be well advised to improve the dissemination of relevant information to the appropriate specialists.[32] This is an infrequently used but potentially important way to prevent obsolescence in the organization. It is only through a well-managed and planned information-utilization program that an organization can be assured of staying abreast of developments relevant to its future viability. Management of knowledge is a functional activity that is becoming increasingly important to the long-range goals of the organization. It should interact closely with the long-range planning and technological forecasting functions so the knowledge needed to meet organizational goals can be determined. How does an organization determine which new developments should be monitored? A general approach has recently been suggested by Peter Drucker:

Technology monitoring is a serious, an important, indeed a vital task. . . . What needs to be watched is "young technology," one that has already had a substantial impact, enough to be judged, to be measured, to be evaluated. And technology monitoring, in respect to the social as well as technological impact of a "young technology," is, above all, a managerial responsibility.[33]

Indeed, it is management's responsibility to determine not only the kind of knowledge required by the organization but also which specific individuals and groups should be kept aware of particular types of knowledge. The knowledge management function must decide how to organize for information retrieval, analysis, diffusion, and utilization in a meaningful fashion. This information can also provide the basis for formal and informal updating programs in the organization. In fact, professionals in organizations in which there are information dissemination functions do keep up to date without wasting time. As one manager says, "We have an excellent means within the company of making people aware, more or less automatically, of what is going on in their field so they don't have to constantly peruse the library literature. This is the dissemination of information system."

The proliferation of computerized information retrieval systems containing knowledge in various fields is one approach to keeping abreast of new developments. Such systems are already available for diverse fields—engineering, chemistry, psychology, and education. Information retrieval can be highly effective when it is integrated with either on-line computer consoles for use by the individual professionals or less sophisticated standard techniques such as routing of articles, reports, and lists of new information sources to the appropriate individuals or groups in the organization. Unless organizations utilize information specialists to serve their professionals much as marketing research specialists provide product-oriented services, organizational obsolescence may be inevitable.

Assess the effectiveness of continuing-education programs. The widespread acceptance of and investment in various continuing-education programs for updating would lead one to believe that some type of evaluation or assessment of these programs would be common.[34] However, all the evidence is to the contrary. Indeed, perhaps the one attribute that most continuing-education programs have in common is the lack of any systematic organizational assessment of their effectiveness.

Assessments that are carried out by some organizations involve various types of criteria or methods, as the following study of over 70 companies found:

> Attitude surveys, skills inventories, turnover analyses and degree and patent counts were identified as ways by which industry assessed the effectiveness and value of its sponsored continuing education. The most frequently used method of assessment was the attitude survey. Degree counts, skills inventories, turnover analyses, and patent counts followed in ranked order. However, more than 60 per cent of the responding companies used no method for assessing either effectiveness or value of their continuing education programs. Collection, analysis, and study of data about objectives, participants, or programs were lacking. This lack of measure and evaluation limited the understanding of means for combatting obsolescence, because it restricted the available knowledge in this field.[35]

Management development programs are a good example of a fad that has been widely accepted despite the fact that few attempts have been made to determine which types of programs are most effective in developing managers. In fact, some organizational researchers are gradually reaching the conclusion "that management development programs should stress factual information and deemphasize techniques of attitudinal change." [36] Nevertheless, most management development programs still focus on human relations training rather than on task-oriented knowledge and skills.

The widely used on-the-job-training approach for professional and management development is another example of a technique whose usefulness for updating may be highly questionable. Management tends to agree, as the following comment by an executive indicates: "On the job training probably is of little value. What is needed is exposure to new ideas, and the stimulation of associating with successful men in other companies and industries. Such exposure and contacts can best be provided by formal development programs such as A.M.A. seminars, etc." [37]

Although organizations tend to recognize the limitations of some types of continuing education, they nevertheless persist in using them. It may well be that they are squandering untold sums of money on updating programs whose sole value is to foster a good public image to help recruit new graduates. One recommendation by researchers who have studied continuing education is that management undertake the evaluation of programs by applying the standard techniques used by personnel researchers for assessing the effects of training. Unfortunately, research techniques have not been applied to the evaluation of continuing education for professionals, and consequently very little is known about the effectiveness of any such type of training or education. Only when organizations begin to apply some type of assessment, preferably in the form of a cost-benefit analysis, to their updating programs, will they be able to determine which types of continuing-education approaches are most effective.

CONTINUING EDUCATION is viewed by both professionals and their organizations as an important way to keep from becoming obsolete. That important role is verified by the $17 billion spent annually by business and industry in educational activities. But despite the enormous allocation of resources to continuing education, it appears that many professionals do not take advantage of available programs. The chief reasons appear to be that they frequently lack the time to take courses and, perhaps more significantly, their organizations neither encourage nor reward professional updating. Even when organizational policies do encourage and reward continuing education, supervisors resist their professional subordinates' diverting time and energy from productive work to course work.

An examination of course modes reveals that the two most prevalent continuing-education methods are (1) graduate-level courses and (2) in-house courses. These two modes appear to serve different purposes and with clear differences in their effects. Graduate-level courses are generally taken by the most capable professionals, and these courses contribute to the maintenance of professional as well as job competence beyond the mid-career. Indeed, they may extend professional usefulness by a decade. On the other hand, in-house courses are typically taken by the less capable professionals because they are less demanding; in fact, it appears that those who are obsolescent in their jobs or professions gravitate toward in-house courses to try to update. However, these courses do not help in reducing obsolescence, partly because of their undemanding nature and partly because they are just too little and too late for some.

Perhaps the most important reason why continuing education has not been more widely successful is that management has not invested enough thought and effort in planning broad integrated updating programs that serve the goals of both the individual and the organization. Several suggestions as to how management can attain that integration have been made:

1. Use the work itself to motivate updating.
2. Assess the continuing-education needs of individual professionals.
3. Provide counseling to guide continuing education.
4. Use innovative techniques to promote self-learning (for example, training by objectives, educational technology, and released time from work).
5. Establish a function to disseminate information to professionals in the organization.
6. Assess the effectiveness of continuing-education programs to determine which modes or combinations of modes are best for particular goals.

The title of this chapter asks whether continuing education is a panacea or a palliative. The answer appears to be that, for most professionals, continuing education by itself is not a panacea for combating obsolescence—at least as long as the work environment and organizational climate do not encourage and reward updating efforts. Until such time as continuing education is integrated with individual and organizational goals, it will be merely a palliative.

Chapter 8

Future Directions

By THIS POINT it should be obvious that obsolescence of knowledge and skills is not only a complex problem but also one that requires an energetic multifaceted effort on the part of the organization to bring it under control. Obsolescence is already a serious problem among technical professionals and managers, as is evidenced by many of the illustrations in this book, and in the decades ahead other organizational professionals will be affected in a similar manner. Despite the ubiquitousness of change and the information explosion, the control of obsolescence as a problem is quite literally in the hands of management. Many suggestions for dealing with obsolescence have been made in the course of this book, and a concise summary of some of them will provide an overall perspective on the future directions organizations can take.

1. Monitor the degree of obsolescence in the organization and establish controls for its detection among individual professionals. Personnel record data, as well as organizational analyses, can be utilized for this purpose, as was described above. The best approaches to monitoring and detecting obsolescence would very likely involve the use of inventories, surveys, or tests of relevant knowledge and skills.

2. Improve techniques of selection and placement to avoid a mismatch of professionals and position requirements. Many standard techniques are available; but regardless of which are

used, it is crucial that they be valid in predicting future obsolescence-relevant behavior.

3. Provide for periodic objective appraisals of future potential and career development. Such techniques as assessment centers, management by objectives, and career counseling can be highly effective in attaining appropriate career development to control obsolescence.

4. Establish a flexible retirement policy and provide for portable pensions. Retirement should be based on the professional's ability to make contributions and not on an arbitrary chronological age. Portable pensions would encourage obsolescent professionals to leave the organization, since they could do so without losing their vesting rights.

5. Redesign professional jobs to make them more challenging. That can be done by improving the utilization of professional knowledge and skills and by increasing individual responsibility and influence. It is most critical that professionals be challenged from their very first job experience in order to stimulate their subsequent growth and development.

6. Provide for changes in job assignments to avoid narrow specialization. Job assignments should require the utilization of different professional knowledge and skills. That would not only help encourage the retention of what the professionals already know but also stimulate the learning of new knowledge and skills and thereby instill confidence that would help the professionals adjust more easily to changing requirements.

7. Allow professionals who have become obsolescent the possibility of a career change. Such a change will typically require the professional to use knowledge and skills that may not be changing as rapidly as those in his original field. One such change can involve moving to an administrative career where accumulated experience, rather than up-to-date professional knowledge, is important. Those who make such a change should receive appropriate management training.

8. Encourage development through colleague interaction by organizing work groups composed of professionals with diverse backgrounds. The composition of such groups should

be changed periodically to provide increased exposure to new ideas and orientations that will serve to stimulate professional growth and development.

9. Select supervisors of professionals primarily on the basis of knowledge and skills that are relevant to the type of work carried out by their subordinates. Professionals are most responsive to leadership when it is backed up by expertise. Techniques used to encourage updating, such as management by objectives, career counseling, and participative management, are effective to the degree that the supervisor's influence is based on his competence.

10. Create an organizational climate through management policies that encourage and reward growth and development. Policies that create open communication and upward influence help to reduce uncertainty about the work as well as problems of utilization and thereby allow for professional growth and development. One way to accomplish this is to make the control system more flexible to allow professionals greater policy-making responsibility, particularly as it pertains to the allocation of resources for reaching work objectives. Individual development can be encouraged if the organization rewards those who maintain their competence with more challenging work, greater responsibility, and influence in policy making. These types of rewards should be accompanied by the more traditional incentives of salary increases and advancement.

11. Carefully plan and evaluate continuing-education programs to help increase their effectiveness in updating professionals. Any type of continuing education will be effective to the degree that it responds to the immediate and long-range needs of the professional. Updating programs that are stimulated and reinforced by the work itself, based on an assessment of education needs, guided by careful counseling, and provided with innovative approaches to promote self-learning are likely to be effective in integrating individual and organizational goals. To attain maximum effectiveness of updating programs, improvements in the management of information

utilization and in the assessment procedures used to determine the efficacy of continuing education are necessary.

Applying Systems Analysis to Updating

It is clear that the above prescriptions may require major changes in management policy and practices. However, even if organizations carefully plan, implement, and monitor the effects of such changes, the complexity of the problem of obsolescence may require more sophisticated responses in the future. There simply are no easy solutions or panaceas. One sophisticated response that has been suggested is to use a systems approach to determine the best strategy for individual updating. Although its use to control obsolescence is still in its infancy, systems analysis may nevertheless be one of the few ways to deal with the many inputs that go into updating. The advantages of such an operation are explained as follows:

> The main advantage of a systems approach is that it enables both the educator and the professional to deal with the various components which promote individual growth and development, taking into account the educational environment, organizational climate, and the psychological factors involved in updating which can be described in a mathematical equation. The systems concept, therefore, provides a framework for visualizing internal and external environmental factors as an integral function. The hypothesis can be stated thus: motivation to update can be simulated as a feedback control system by utilizing a mathematical model which incorporates the motivational and personality variables, the educational environment, and organizational factors.[1]

Although the systems analysis approach is still quite rudimentary and incomplete, it does attempt to deal with the complex interrelationships among the multiple inputs that stimulate updating, and promises to provide optimal methods of obsolescence control. However, that may be far in the future, since a great deal more must be learned about obsolescence before sophisticated systems analysis models can be effectively used in its control.

A Center for Obsolescence Research

It is obvious that more research on obsolescence is needed before organizations are going to make any major commitment of resources to innovative, but unproved, techniques. Management should have learned the lesson that, just because it has become faddish in dealing with a problem, a particular technique does not necessarily work. Perhaps it would be worthwhile for organizations to seriously consider the concluding proposal presented at the First Conference on Occupational Obsolescence, which called for the establishment of a center for obsolescence research. The reasons for establishing such a center were described by the participants as follows:

> It was felt that there was a need for more valid information, which could be used by different enterprises to prevent and combat obsolescence. Individual companies and other organizations, although doing research related to this subject with their own staffs, really could not gear up to a broad, comprehensive, comparative, longitudinal research program without considerable additional staff and budget. One way of expanding the research would be to establish an independent research group, supported by various organizations interested in obsolescence, that would supplement the research now being carried out by individual organizations.[2]

The proposal went on to describe the center as being able to: [3]

1. Perform the research needed, but not being performed, by individual companies and other organizations.
2. Serve as a clearinghouse for research in obsolescence for member companies and other organizations.
3. Provide consultation to member companies and other organizations.
4. Stimulate new research in human obsolescence.
5. Issue periodic reports on the status of research in human obsolescence.

The proposal also provided descriptions of the characteristics of the group doing the research, the problems in which the group should engage, and the structure and financing of the center. It was suggested that the research group should be knowledgeable about organizational problems and economic growth and development; it should be independent of any company or industry to assure objectivity in the research; and it should be multidisciplinary, including applied researchers in such areas as psychology, economics, sociology, anthropology, physiology, and other sciences pertinent to the study of obsolescence. Some of the areas of research that were believed to be most important include studies and evaluations of careers, educational preparation, retraining, job rotation, specific management practice, corporate structure, and existing antiobsolescence measures thought to be successful.

According to the proposal, the center's advisory board should consist of representatives of member organizations that are contributing to the funding of the center. The advisory board should help select research problems that are considered most pressing. The establishing of a center of obsolescence research appears to be a highly promising activity on which organizations can focus their efforts. However, such a center should not be totally dependent on business and industry for support, since its activities will also be relevant to professional societies and associations, institutions of higher learning, and the federal government.

PROFESSIONAL SOCIETIES AND ASSOCIATIONS

The various professional societies and associations have long recognized the need for updating among their members, and many of them have sponsored formal continuing-education programs. In fact, professionals generally find society courses to be the most appealing of all formal continuing-education modes for updating in their current work. Therefore, it would be in the interest of the professional societies and associations to utilize a center for obsolescence research not only to assist in the development and evaluation of society-sponsored continuing-education programs and to act as a central clearinghouse of such activities but also to help determine policy on such relevant issues as professional licensing and relicensing. Professions such as architecture, medicine, law, pharmacy, psychology, and teaching require a demonstration of proficiency before they permit their members to practice. Even some technical and business specialists such as engineers and accountants also are required to pass a proficiency examination prior to being permitted to take on certain professional responsibilities.

To protect consumers of professional services by assuring the continuing competency of professionals, it is not too unreasonable to demand that specialists, in order to maintain their professional standing, demonstrate that they have stayed up to date with the knowledge and skills in their fields. Perhaps a harbinger of things to come is the case of eleven physicians who were suspended from membership in the Oregon Medical Association for failure to keep up with educational requirements and thereby lost their membership in the American Medical Association.[4] The requirements involved a demonstration that members spend approximately 50 hours annually in continuing education and professional activities, which were broadly defined to include formal reading programs, teaching, preparation of professional papers, and publication of articles requiring study and research. Several professional groups are discussing similar requirements for their members. A center for obsolescence research could serve the professional societies and associations in assessing the need for and the potential impact of such policy decisions in various fields.

By including representatives of concerned professional associations on the advisory board, the center for obsolescence research would provide an opportunity for these associations to interact with the employers of their members. In that manner, an attempt could be made to integrate the goals of the profession with those of the organizations that require the services of professionals.

PROFESSIONAL SCHOOLS

Although the value of graduate-level courses was discussed in the section on continuing education (see Chapter 7), little was said of how the role of the professional schools can be improved. After all, the professional schools do play the major role in formal updating programs, not only by sponsoring courses but also by providing teachers for in-house courses. It has been suggested that graduate-level continuing-education programs be made more relevant by relocating the programs into the organizations that employ or will employ the professionals taking the courses.[5] This and other such innovations could more easily be made if representatives of professional schools that sponsor continuing education were included in a center for obsolescence research. By providing an interface between the professional schools and the organizations utilizing their services, more effective educational standards, practices, and technology can be attained and collaborative arrangements for both on-campus and in-house programs between employers and schools can be improved for their mutual benefit. In this way professional education will stay updated and relevant to the future.

FEDERAL GOVERNMENT

All levels of government sponsor updating programs for their professionals, and the federal government has placed a great emphasis on in-house courses. Government involvement in the center would be quite appropriate not only to improve the development of government professionals but also to serve as a major source of research support. Government funding for obsolescence research would be highly appropriate, since maintenance of knowledge and skills among professional workers in general is directly related to the ability of the United States to maintain its leadership in a rapidly changing and increasingly competitive world.

OTHER INTERESTED GROUPS

Participation in, as well as support for, a center for obsolescence research need not be limited to the groups mentioned thus far. Clearly, private foundations and trade associations have a role to play. However, since the proposal is future-directed, the details of membership and operations should be left broad and open-ended until those most concerned about the problem decide to establish a center for obsolescence research.

A Final Word

This book has primarily been concerned with understanding the causes of and prescribing cures for the obsolescence of knowledge and skills among professionals. The focus has been on the role of the organization in creating, as well as overcoming, obsolescence. Since management bears much of the onus for allowing obsolescence to occur, it is only just that it bear the primary responsibility for providing the conditions that will facilitate professional development. This is in management's own interest, but it can do no more than create a climate which encourages and rewards the continuous maintenance of competence. The rest is up to the individual, upon whom rests the ultimate responsibility for life-long learning and professional career development.

REFERENCES

Chapter 1

1. For a more extensive discussion of the impact of change see P. F. Drucker, *The Age of Discontinuity* (New York: Harper & Row, 1969) and A. Toffler, *Future Shock* (New York: Random House, 1970).

2. The statistics for R&D and education expenditures were obtained from A. O. Stanley and K. K. White, *Organizing the R&D Function,* AMA Research Study 72 (1965); *National Patterns of R&D Resources: Funds and Manpower in the United States 1953–70,* NSF 69-30 (1969), National Science Foundation, Washington, D.C.; K. A. Simon and W. V. Grant, *Digest of Educational Statistics, 1970 Edition,* U.S. Department of Health, Education and Welfare, Washington, D.C., September 1970.

3. The emergence of a "knowledge economy" is discussed by Drucker, op. cit.

4. The concepts of "knowledge industries" and "knowledge workers" have been rather broadly defined and extensively analyzed by A. Machlup, *The Production and Distribution of Knowledge in the United States* (Princeton, N.J.: Princeton University Press, 1962).

5. The employment statistics utilized in this section have been obtained from the following U.S. Department of Labor publications unless otherwise noted: *Occupational Outlook Handbook,* 1972–1973 edition, Bureau of Labor Statistics, Bulletin 1700; *College Educated Workers, 1968–80,* Bureau of Labor Statistics, Bulletin 1676 (1970); *The U.S. Economy in 1980: A Summary of BLS Projections,* Bureau of Labor Statistics, Bulletin 1673 (1970); R. B. Elanders, "Employment Patterns for the 1970's," *Occupational Outlook Quarterly,* Vol. 14 (1970), No.

2, pp. 2–17; D. F. Johnston, "Education of Adult Workers: Projections to 1985," *Monthly Labor Review*, Vol. 93 (August 1970), pp. 43–56.

6. Drucker, op. cit. (ref. 1).

7. See surveys discussed by J. M. Gould, *The Technical Elite* (New York: Kelley, 1966).

8. National Science Foundation, *Employment of Scientists and Engineers in the United States 1950–66*, NSF 68-30, 1968.

9. Gould, op. cit. (ref. 7).

10. R. D. Bradish, "Accountants in Top Management," *The Journal of Accountancy*, Vol. 129 (June 1970), pp. 49–51.

11. D. Kaye, "Career Path in Systems and Data Processing," *Journal of Systems Management*, Vol. 22 (1971), No. 6, pp. 12–15.

12. Data pertaining to the information explosion appear in the following sources: J. B. Bennett and R. L. Weiher, "The Well-Read Manager," *Harvard Business Review*, Vol. 50 (July-August 1972), No. 4, pp. 134–146; R. Perrucci and R. A. Rothman, "Obsolescence of Knowledge and the Professional Career," in R. Perrucci and J. E. Gerstl (Eds.), *The Engineers and the Social System* (New York: Wiley, 1969); Toffler, op. cit. (ref. 1).

13. D. J. de Solla Price, *Science Since Babylon* (New Haven, Conn.: Yale University Press, 1961), p. 97.

14. The data on information acquisition among technical professionals were obtained from Case Institute of Technology Operations Research Group, *An Operations Research Study of the Scientific Activity of Chemists* (Cleveland: Case Institute of Technology, 1958); C. W. Hanson, "Research on Users' Needs: Where Is It Getting Us?" *ASLIB Proceedings*, Vol. 16 (February 1964), pp. 64–78; J. R. Hinrichs, "Communications Activity of Industrial Research Personnel," *Personnel Psychology*, Vol. 17 (1964), pp. 193–204; I. H. Hogg and J. R. Smith, "Information and Literature Use in a Research and Development Organization," in *Proceedings of the International Conference on Scientific Information* (Washington, D.C.: National Academy of Science, 1959); M. W. Martin, Jr., "The Use of Random Alarm Devices in Studying Scientists' Reading Behavior," *IRE Transactions on Engineering Management*, Vol. EM-9 (1962), No. 2, pp. 66–71; R. S. Rosenbloom and F. W. Wolek, *Technology and Information Transfer: A Survey of Practice in*

Industrial Organizations (Boston: Harvard University Press, 1970).
The data on information acquisition among managers were obtained from S. S. Dubin, E. Alderman, and H. L. Marlow, *Managerial and Supervisory Needs of Business and Industry in Pennsylvania* (University Park, Pa.: Department of Planning Studies, Continuing Education, Pennsylvania State University, 1967); S. Carlson, *Executive Behavior: A Study of the Work Load and the Working Methods of Managing Directors* (Stockholm: Stromberghs, 1951); J. M. Horne and T. Lupton, "The Work Activities of 'Middle' Managers: An Exploratory Study," *Journal of Management Studies,* Vol. 2 (February 1965), pp. 14–33; W. J. Stewart, "Determining First-Line Supervisory Training Needs," *Training and Development Journal,* Vol. 24 (April 1970), pp. 12–19.

15. J. L. George and S. S. Dubin, *Continuing Education Needs of Natural Resource Managers and Scientists* (University Park, Pa.: Department of Planning Studies, Continuing Education, Pennsylvania State University, 1972).

16. S. S. Dubin and H. L. Marlow, "Keeping Up to Date: Replies from 2090 Engineers," paper presented at a meeting of the American Society for Engineering Education, University of Maine, 1964; George and Dubin, op. cit. (ref. 15); R. Renck, *Continuing Education for R&D Careers,* NSF 69-20, National Science Foundation, June 1969; Rosenbloom and Wolek, op. cit. (ref. 14); Bureau of National Affairs, "Tools of the Personnel Profession," *Personnel Policies Forum* (No. 93) (March 1971).

17. T. K. Glennan, "Inventing an Education for Engineers," *Saturday Review,* Vol. 48 (November 20, 1965), No. 1, p. 94.

Chapter 2

1. J. G. Roney, *Report on First Conference on Occupational Obsolescence* (Menlo Park, Calif.: Stanford Research Institute, 1966).

2. Research studies focusing on technical obsolescence included in the analysis of definitions were the following: T. N. Ferdinand, "On the Obsolescence of Scientists and Engineers," *American Scientist,* Vol. 54 (1966), No. 1, pp. 45–56; P. Mali, "Measurement of Obsolescence in Engineering Practitioners," *Manage,* Vol. 21 (1969), No. 5, pp. 48–52; P. H. Norgren,

"Obsolescence and Updating of Engineers' and Scientists' Skills," Columbia University, *Seminar on Technology and Social Change* (November 1966); R. Perrucci and R. A. Rothman, "Obsolescence of Knowledge and the Professional Career," in R. Perrucci and J. E. Gerstl (Eds.), *The Engineers and the Social System* (New York: Wiley, 1969), pp. 247–275; Stanford Research Institute, *Technical Manpower Obsolescence* (Menlo Park, Calif.: Stanford Research Institute, 1968a). Investigations of managerial obsolescence included the following: L. M. Cone, Jr., "Toward a Theory of Managerial Obsolescence: An Empirical and Theoretical Study," doctoral dissertation, New York University, 1968; F. C. Haas, *Executive Obsolescence,* AMA Research Study 90 (1968); Stanford Research Institute, *Managerial Obsolescence* (Menlo Park, Calif.: Stanford Research Institute, 1968b).

3. R. Renck, *Continuing Education for R & D Careers,* NSF 69-20, National Science Foundation, June 1969, p. 5.

4. Information on obsolescence among technical professionals was obtained from Mali, op. cit. (ref. 2); Norgren, op. cit. (ref. 2); Perrucci and Rothman, op. cit. (ref. 2); E. Raudsepp, "Engineers Talk About Obsolescence," *Machine Design,* Vol. 36 (June 18, 1964), pp. 148–151; E. Raudsepp, "Engineers Predict Problems of the 70's," *Machine Design,* Vol. 38 (March 3, 1966a), pp. 93–99; E. Raudsepp, "Keeping Up with New Knowledge," *Machine Design,* Vol. 38 (March 31, 1966b), pp. 93–99; "Eighty-nine Percent of Scientists and Engineers Face 'Technical Obsolescence,' " *Industrial Research,* Vol. 15 (1967), cited by Renck, op. cit., p. 6; R. R. Ritti, *The Engineer in the Industrial Corporation* (New York: Columbia University Press, 1971); and Stanford Research Institute, op. cit. (ref. 2), 1968a.

5. Information on obsolescence among salaried managers was obtained from E. H. Burack and G. C. Pati, "Technology and Managerial Obsolescence," *MSU Business Topics,* Vol. 18 (September 1970), pp. 49–56; Cone, op. cit. (ref. 2); M. J. Gannon and J. P. Noon, "Management's Critical Deficiency," *Business Horizons* (February 1971), pp. 49–56; J. E. Genders, "How to Cope with the Obsolescent Executive," *Personnel Management,* Vol. 3 (October 1971), pp. 26–28; Mali, op. cit. (ref. 2); R. A. Rothman, "Knowledge Obsolescence Among

Professionals: A Study of Career, Personal and Organizational Factors Related to Technical Obsolescence Among Engineers," doctoral dissertation, Purdue University, 1969; J. R. Hinrichs, "Applying Motivational Concepts to Updating," paper presented as part of symposium on motivation for professional updating at the International Congress of Applied Psychology, Liege, Belgium, July 1971; Raudsepp, op. cit. (ref. 4), 1964; Raudsepp, op. cit. (ref. 4), 1966a; Raudsepp, op. cit., 1966b; and Stanford Research Institute, op. cit. (ref. 4), 1968b.

6. Information on other organizational professionals was obtained from Hinrichs, op. cit., 1971, and Stanford Research Institute, op. cit. (ref. 2), 1968a.

7. Ritti, op. cit. (ref. 4), p. 216.

8. The critical incident approach applied to obsolescence is described in H. G. Kaufman, "A Critical Incident Study of Personal Characteristics Associated with Technical Obsolescence Among Engineers," *Studies in Personnel Psychology,* Vol. 5 (1973), No. 1, pp. 63–67.

9. The example of the knowledge survey is taken from Perrucci and Rothman, op. cit. (ref. 2).

10. Mali, op. cit. (ref. 2), pp. 49–50.

11. Gannon and Noon, op. cit. (ref. 5).

12. Information on the job knowledge survey was provided by T. J. Hartford, Assistant Director, Division of Executive Development, Graduate School of Business, University of Pittsburgh.

Chapter 3

1. J. F. Roney, *Report on First Conference on Occupational Obsolescence* (Menlo Park, Calif.: Stanford Research Institute, August 1966), p. 5.

2. J. P. Jordon, *How Are Age and Technical Changes Affecting Employment of Executives?* AMA Personnel Series, No. 2 (1930); E. D. Smith, *What Are the Psychological Factors of Obsolescence of Workers in Middle Age?* AMA Personnel Series, No. 9 (1930).

3. F. C. Haas, *Executive Obsolescence,* AMA Research Study 90 (1968).

4. G. W. Dalton and P. H. Thompson, "Accelerating Obsolescence

of Older Engineers," *Harvard Business Review,* Vol. 49 (September-October 1971), No. 5, pp. 57–67.

5. These types of relationships have been reported in several research studies including H. C. Lehman, *Age and Achievement* (Princeton, N.J.: Princeton University Press, 1963); Dalton and Thompson, op. cit.; and P. Mali, "Measurement of Obsolescence in Engineering Practitioners," *Manage,* Vol. 21 (1969), No. 5, pp. 48–52.

6. See, for example, studies by R. J. Burke, "Effects of Aging on Engineer's Satisfactions and Mental Health: Skill Obsolescence," *Academy of Management Journal,* Vol. 12 (December 1969), pp. 478–486; R. P. Loomba, "A Study of the Re-employment and Employment Experiences of Scientists and Engineers Laid Off from 62 Aerospace and Electronics Firms in the San Francisco Bay Area During 1963–1965," Manpower Research Group, Center for Interdisciplinary Studies, San Jose State College, February 15, 1967; J. D. Mooney, "An Analysis of Unemployment Among Professional Engineers and Scientists," *Industrial and Labor Relations Review,* Vol. 19 (1966), pp. 517–528; R. L. Turmail, "Compare Your Career with Your Peers," *Electronic Design* (April 27, 1972), pp. 42–47.

7. Such relationships were reported by W. Dennis, "Age and Productivity Among Scientists," *Science,* Vol. 23 (1956), pp. 724–725; Bernice Eiduson, "Productivity Rate in Research Scientists," *American Scientist,* Vol. 54 (1966), No. 1, pp. 57–63; W. Oberg, "Age and Achievement and the Technical Man," *Personnel Psychology,* Vol. 13 (1960), pp. 245–284; Naomi Stuart and W. J. Sparks, "Patent Productivity of Research Chemists as Related to Age and Experience," *Personnel and Guidance Journal,* Vol. 45 (1966), pp. 28–36.

8. Twin-peaked relationships are reported by Oberg, op. cit.; D. Pelz, "The Creative Years and the Research Environment," *IEEE Transactions on Engineering Management,* Vol. EM-11 (1964), pp. 23–29; D. Pelz and F. M. Andrews, *Scientists in Organizations* (New York: Wiley, 1966).

9. Research into the mid-career crisis has been described in articles such as "Three Phases of Adulthood: Transitions Termed as Difficult as Adolescence," *New York Times,* July 11, 1971, p. 41; "Mid-Life Viewed as Crisis Period," *New York Times,* November 19, 1972, p. 51; H. Levinson, "On Being a Middle-

Aged Manager," *Harvard Business Review,* Vol. 47 (July-August 1969), pp. 51–60.

10. P. H. Norgren, "Obsolescence and Updating of Engineers' and Scientists' Skills," Columbia University, *Seminar on Technology and Social Change* (November 1966), p. 59.

11. U.S. Department of Labor, *The Employment Problems of Old Workers,* Bureau of Labor Statistics, Bulletin 1721, 1971.

12. S. S. Dubin, "Obsolescence or Lifelong Education: A Choice for the Professional," *American Psychologist,* Vol. 27 (May 1972), No. 5, p. 486.

13. See S. B. Zelikoff, "On the Obsolescence and Retraining of Engineering Personnel," *Training and Development Journal,* Vol. 23 (May 1969), pp. 3–15.

14. Norgren, op. cit. (ref. 10), p. 58.

15. See S. Cenko, "Factors in Obsolescence of Engineering Knowledge," master's thesis, Sloan School of Management, MIT, 1964; R. Perrucci and R. A. Rothman, "Obsolescence of Knowledge and the Professional Career," in R. Perrucci and J. E. Gerstl (Eds.), *The Engineers and the Social System* (New York: Wiley, 1969).

16. The importance of cognitive abilities is reported by J. P. Campbell, M. D. Dunnette, E. L. Lawler, and K. E. Weick, *Managerial Behavior, Performance and Effectiveness* (New York: McGraw-Hill, 1970); Cenko, op. cit.; Haas, op. cit. (ref. 3); J. K. Hemphill (Ed.), *The Engineering Study* (Princeton, N.J.: Educational Testing Service, 1963); H. G. Kaufman, "Relations of Ability and Interest to Currency of Professional Knowledge Among Engineers," *Journal of Applied Psychology,* Vol. 56 (1972), pp. 495–499; H. G. Kaufman, "A Critical Incident Study of Personal Characteristics Associated with Technical Obsolescence Among Engineers," *Studies in Personnel Psychology,* Vol. 5 (1973), No. 1, pp. 63–67; A. K. Korman, Marie B. Antonelli, R. D. Singer, and Adele F. FeKete, "The Generality of the Characteristics of 'Competent' People," *Journal of Vocational Behavior,* Vol. 1 (1971), pp. 201–208; E. M. Rogers, *Diffusion of Innovations* (New York: Free Press of Glencoe, 1962).

17. This discussion of age and ability is based primarily on that presented by J. B. Minor, *Personnel Psychology* (New York: Macmillan, 1969), and by the National Council on the Aging,

Utilization of Older Professional and Scientific Workers (New York: National Council on the Aging, 1961).

18. Information on motivation was obtained from J. Hinrichs, "Applying Motivational Concepts to Updating," paper presented at the International Congress of Applied Psychology, Liege, Belgium, July 1971; Kaufman, op. cit. (ref. 16), 1973; Pelz and Andrews, op. cit. (ref. 8).

19. Norgren, op. cit. (ref. 10), p. 59.

20. Information on interests was obtained from D. R. Benjamin, "A Thirty-one-Year Longitudinal Study of Engineering Students' Interest Profiles and Career Patterns," doctoral dissertation, Purdue University, 1967; Campbell et al., op. cit. (ref. 16); M. D. Dunnette, P. Wernimont, and N. Abrahams, "Further Research and Vocational Interest Differences Among Several Types of Engineers," *Personnel and Guidance Journal*, Vol. 42 (1964), pp. 484–493; Hemphill, op. cit. (ref. 16); Kaufman, op. cit. (ref. 16), 1972; Kaufman, op. cit. (ref. 16), 1973.

21. Information on needs was obtained from D. T. Hall and K. E. Nougaim, "An Examination of Maslow's Need Hierarchy in an Organizational Setting," *Organizational Behavior and Human Performance*, Vol. 3 (1968), pp. 12–35; Korman et al., op. cit. (ref. 16); R. G. Kuhlen, "Developmental Changes in Motivation During the Adult Years," in J. E. Birren (Ed.), *Relations of Development and Aging* (Springfield, Ill.: Thomas, 1964); D. C. McClelland, *The Achieving Society* (Princeton, N.J.: Van Nostrand, 1961); R. A. Rothman, "Knowledge Obsolescence Among Professionals," doctoral dissertation, Purdue University, 1969.

22. Information on goals was obtained from the author's own data and the following sources: "Student Attitudes Toward Industry," *Personnel Journal*, Vol. 49 (June 1970), pp. 517–519; O. Behling and H. H. Rodkin, "How College Students Find Jobs: A National Survey," *Personnel Administration*, Vol. 32 (September-October 1969), pp. 35–42; L. C. Goldberg, F. Baker, and A. M. Rubenstein, "Local-Cosmopolitan: Unidimensional or Multidimensional," *American Journal of Sociology*, Vol. 70 (May 1965), pp. 704–710; F. H. Goldner, "Success vs. Failure: Prior Managerial Perspectives," *Industrial Relations*, Vol. 9 (October 1970), pp. 453–474; L. Goodwin, "Occupational Goals and Satisfactions of the American Work Force," *Per-*

sonnel Psychology, Vol. 22 (1969), pp. 313–325; J. R. Hinrichs, "The Attitudes of Research Chemists," *Journal of Applied Psychology*, Vol. 48 (1964), pp. 287–293; Kuhlen, op cit.; F. Landis, "What Makes Technical Men Happy and Productive?" *Research Management*, Vol. 14 (May 1971), pp. 24–42; R. R. Ritti, *The Engineer in the Industrial Corporation* (New York: Columbia University Press, 1971), chaps. 3 and 4; G. W. Trump and H. S. Hendrickson, "Job Selection Preferences of Accounting Students," *Journal of Accountancy*, Vol. 129 (June 1970), pp. 84–86.

23. Studies that discuss energy include those by Haas, op. cit.; T. W. Harrel, *Follow-up of Management Potential Battery* (Stanford, Calif.: Stanford University Press, 1967); Kulen, op. cit. (ref. 21); R. G. Morrison, W. A. Owens, J. R. Glennon, and L. E. Albright, "Factored Life History Antecedents of Industrial Research Performance," *Journal of Applied Psychology*, Vol. 46 (1962), pp. 251–284; D. E. Robertson, "Dealing with Unpromotable Managers," *Business Perspectives*, Vol. 8 (1972), No. 13; and Anne Roe, "A Psychological Study of Physical Scientists," *Genetic Psychology Monographs*, Vol. 43 (Second Half) (1951), pp. 121–239.

24. Initiative has been discussed by J. A. Chambers, "Relating Personality and Biographical Factors to Scientific Creativity," *Psychological Monographs*, Vol. 78 (No. 7, Serial Whole No. 584, 1964); W. R. Dill, "Obsolescence as a Problem of Personal Initiative," in S. S. Dubin (Ed.), *Professional Obsolescence* (Lexington, Mass.: Heath, 1972); E. E. Ghiselli, "Correlates of Initiative," *Personnel Psychology*, Vol. 9 (1956), pp. 311–320; Harrel, op. cit.

25. F. J. Gaudet and A. R. Carli, "Why Executives Fail," *Personnel Psychology*, Vol. 10 (1957), pp. 7–21.

26. Information on the self-concept is found in D. T. Hall, "A Theoretical Model of Career Subidentity Development in Organizational Settings," *Organizational Behavior and Human Performance*, Vol. 6 (1971), pp. 50–76; Harrell, op. cit. (ref. 23); Haas, op. cit. (ref. 3); A. K. Korman, *Industrial and Organizational Psychology* (Englewood Cliffs, N.J.: Prentice-Hall, 1971); Kuhlen, op. cit. (ref. 21); D. A. Seiler, *Job Adjustment and Satisfaction During the Professional's First*

Year of Employment (Princeton, N.J.: Western Electric Company, 1971).

27. Information on risk taking was obtained from C. Argyris, *Organization and Innovation* (Homewood, Ill.: Irwin-Dorsey, 1965); N. George and T. U. Embse, "Leadership Attitudes," *Manage* (December 1970), pp. 6–11; Haas, op. cit. (ref. 3); G. L. Litwin and J. A. Ciarlo, *Achievement Motivation and Risk-Taking in a Business Setting* (New York: Behavioral Research Services, General Electric Company, 1951); V. H. Vroom and B. Pahl, "Relationship Between Age and Risk-Taking Among Managers," *Journal of Applied Psychology*, Vol. 55 (1971), pp. 399–405; L. K. Williams, "Some Correlates of Risk Taking," *Personnel Psychology*, Vol. 18 (1965), pp. 297–310.

28. Rogers, op. cit. (ref. 16), p. 169.

29. Information on rigidity and flexibility has been obtained from M. D. Dunnette and M. S. Aylward, "Validity Information Exchange No. 9–20"; D.O.T. Code, "Design & Development Engineers," *Personnel Psychology*, Vol. 9 (1956), pp. 245–247; Haas, op. cit. (ref. 3); D. W. MacKinnon, "The Nature and Nurture of Creative Talent," *American Psychologist*, Vol. 17 (1962), pp. 481–495; Rogers, op. cit. (ref. 16); K. W. Schaie and C. R. Strother, "The Effect of Time and Cohort Differences on the Interpretation of Age Changes in Cognitive Behavior," *Multivariate Behavioral Research*, Vol. 3 (1968), pp. 259–294.

30. D. E. Berlew and D. T. Hall, "The Socialization of Managers: Effects of Expectations on Performance," *Administrative Science Quarterly*, Vol. 11 (1966), pp. 207–223; F. C. Mann and F. W. Neff, *Managing Major Change in Organizations* (Ann Arbor, Mich: The Foundation for Research on Human Behavior, 1961).

Chapter 4

1. For information on selection and placement of professionals see J. R. Hinrichs, *High-Talent Personnel: Managing a Critical Resource* (AMA, 1965).

2. D. L. Billiet, et al., "Top Management Looks at Loss of Motivation, Overpromotion, Manager Obsolescence," Graduate School of Business, Stanford University, August 1961, p. 52.

3. Ibid., p. 53.

4. For an overview of the strengths and weaknesses of various assessment and counseling techniques see W. Oberg, "Make Performance Appraisal Relevant," *Harvard Business Review,* Vol. 50 (January-February 1972), pp. 61–67.

5. For a review of the potential of assessment centers see A. I. Kraut, "A Hard Look at Management Assessment Centers and Their Future," *Personnel Journal,* Vol. 51 (1972), No. 5, pp. 317–326.

6. MBO applied to the problem of obsolescence is described by R. B. Easton, "Arresting Executive Obsolescence and Organizational Decay," *Hospital Administration,* Vol. 15 (1970), No. 4, pp. 28–39; and N. J. Horgan and R. P. Floyd, "An MBO Approach to Prevent Technical Obsolescence," *Personnel Journal,* Vol. 50 (1971), No. 9, pp. 686–692.

7. Counseling and mid-career change are discussed by S. S. Dubin, "Obsolescence or Lifelong Education: A Choice for the Professional," *American Psychologist,* Vol. 27 (1972), No. 5, pp. 416–498. Career paths are discussed by J. J. Wnuk, "Career Paths," *Training and Development Journal,* Vol. 24 (1970), No. 5, pp. 38–40.

8. Information on retirement was obtained from G. E. Bates, "A Fresh Look at Retirement," *Harvard Business School Bulletin* (January-February 1971), pp. 14–19; M. R. Greene, H. C. Pyron, U. V. Manion, and H. Winkleross, *Early Retirement: A Survey of Company Policies and Retirees' Experiences* (Eugene, Oreg.: College of Business Administration, University of Oregon, 1969); A. Monk, "Factors in the Preparation for Retirement by Middle Aged Adults," doctoral dissertation, Brandeis University, 1970; S. D. Saleh, "A Study of Attitude Change in the Preretirement Period," *Journal of Applied Psychology,* Vol. 48 (1964), No. 5, pp. 310–312.

9. Bates, op. cit., p. 15.

10. Ibid., p. 17.

11. Monk, op. cit. (ref. 8), p. 233.

Chapter 5

1. J. G. Roney, *Report on the First Conference on Occupational Obsolescence* (Menlo Park, Calif.: Stanford Research Institute, August 1966), p. 2.

2. Ibid., p. 7.

3. W. A. Owens, "Age and Mental Abilities: A Second Adult Follow-up," *Journal of Educational Psychology*, Vol. 57 (1966), pp. 311–325.

4. Results of the management progress study were obtained from D. E. Berlow and D. T. Hall, "The Socialization of Managers: Effects of Expectations on Performance," *Administrative Science Quarterly*, Vol. 11 (1966), pp. 207–224; R. J. Campbell, "Career Development: The Young Business Manager," paper presented at the meeting of the American Psychological Association, San Francisco, 1968; "Management Progress Study: Some Early Results," Personnel Relations Department, Bell System, October 1965.

5. H. G. Kaufman, "Work Environment, Personal Characteristics and Obsolescence of Engineers," grant 91-34-69-23, Department of Labor, Office of Manpower Management, June 1970, Clearinghouse for Federal Scientific and Technical Information Report PB 192273.

6. D. T. Hall, "Potential for Career Growth," *Personnel Administration*, Vol. 34 (1971), No. 3, pp. 18–30.

7. The two types of utilization are thoroughly discussed by R. R. Ritti, *The Engineer in the Industrial Corporation* (New York: Columbia University Press, 1971). Excerpts from this work are reprinted by permission of the publisher.

8. Ibid., p. 105.

9. Ibid., p. 217.

10. Ibid., p. 98.

11. For the effects of time and quality pressure see F. M. Andrews and G. F. Farris, "Time Pressure and Performance of Scientists and Engineers: A Five Year Panel Study," *Organizational Behavior and Human Performance*, Vol. 8 (1972), pp. 185–200; D. T. Hall and E. E. Lawler, "Job Characteristics and Pressures and the Organizational Integration of the Professionals," *Administrative Science Quarterly*, Vol. 15 (1970), pp. 271–281.

12. See R. A. Rothman and R. Perrucci, "Organization Careers and Professional Expertise," *Administrative Science Quarterly*, Vol. 15 (1970), No. 3, pp. 282–293; Stanford Research Institute, *Technical Manpower Obsolescence* (Menlo Park, Calif.: Stanford Research Institute, 1968).

13. R. Lindsey, "Rapid Transit and Aerospace," *New York Times*, December 10, 1972, sec. 3, p. 5.

14. E. E. Lawler, "How Long Should a Manager Stay in the Same Job?" *Personnel Administration* (September-October 1964), pp. 7–8, 27.
15. E. E. Ghiselli, "Correlates of Initiative," *Personnel Psychology*, Vol. 9 (1956), pp. 319–320.
16. R. R. Ritti, *Engineers and Managers: A Study of Engineering Organization*, doctoral dissertation, Cornell University, 1960, p. 142.
17. Ibid.
18. Rothman and Perrucci, op. cit. (ref. 12), p. 291.
19. T. N. Ferdinand, "On the Obsolescence of Scientists and Engineers," *American Scientist*, Vol. 54 (1966), No. 1, p. 51.
20. N. Margulies and A. P. Raia, "Scientists, Engineers and Technological Obsolescence," *California Management Review*, Vol. 10 (1967), No. 2, p. 44.
21. Ferdinand, op. cit. (ref. 19), p. 53.
22. Stanford Research Institute, op. cit. (ref. 12).
23. The originator of the term "formatted tasks" was Dr. R. Miller, who carried out research on obsolescence at the IBM Corporation.
24. F. Landis, "What Makes Technical Man Happy and Productive?" *Research Management*, Vol. 14 (May 1971), p. 28.
25. R. R. Ritti, "Job Enrichment and Skill Utilization in Engineering Organizations," in J. R. Maher (Ed.), *New Perspectives in Job Enrichment* (New York: Van Nostrand Reinhold, 1971), p. 147.
26. D. Harris and F. Chaney, "Human Factors in Quality Assurance," No. P7-2787/501, November 2, 1967, Autonetics Division of North American Rockwell, Anaheim, Calif.
27. W. J. Paul, K. B. Robertson, and F. Herzberg, "Job Enrichment Pays Off," *Harvard Business Review*, Vol. 47 (March-April 1969), pp. 61–78.

Chapter 6

1. The information on colleague interaction and communication was obtained from the author's own data and the following sources: T. J. Allen, "Roles in Technical Communication Networks," MIT Sloan School Working Papers 434–69, December 1969; S. S. Dubin, E. Alderman, and H. L. Marlow, *Managerial and Supervisory Educational Needs of Business and Industry in Pennsylvania* (University Park, Pa.: Department of Planning

Studies, Continuing Education, Pennsylvania State University, 1967); R. S. Rosenbloom and F. W. Wolek, *Technology and Information Transfer* (Boston: Division of Research, Graduate School of Business Administration, Harvard University, 1970); N. Margulies and A. Raia, "Scientists, Engineers and Technological Obsolescence," *California Management Review*, Vol. 10 (1967), No. 2, pp. 43–48; D. C. Pelz and F. M. Andrews, *Scientists in Organizations* (New York: Wiley, 1960); R. Renck, *Continuing Education for R&D Careers*, NSF 69-20 (Washington, D.C.: National Science Foundation, 1969); C. G. Smith, "Age of R&D Groups: A Reconsideration," *Human Relations*, Vol. 23 (1970), No. 2, pp. 81–96.

2. Margulies and Raia, op. cit., p. 44.

3. The information on leadership style and expertise was obtained from the author's own data and the following sources: F. M. Andrews and G. F. Farris, "Supervisory Practices and Innovation in Scientific Teams," *Personnel Psychology*, Vol. 20 (1967), No. 4, pp. 497–515; Stephen C. Hill, "A Natural Experiment on the Influence of Leadership Behavior Patterns on Scientific Productivity," *IEEE Transactions on Engineering Management*, Vol. EM-17 (1970), No. 1, pp. 10–20; J. W. Slocum, "Supervisory Influence and the Professional Employee," *Personnel Journal*, Vol. 49 (1970), No. 6, pp. 484–488; M. Patchen, "The Locus and Basis of Influence on Organizational Decisions," Working Paper no. 37, Institute for the Study of Social Change, Department of Sociology, Purdue University; Renck, op. cit.; G. Graen, F. Dansereau, and T. Minam, "An Empirical Test of the Man-in-the-Middle Hypothesis Among Executives in a Hierarchical Organization Employing a Unit-Set Analysis," *Organizational Behavior and Human Performance*, Vol. 8 (1972), pp. 262–285.

4. E. Raudsepp, "How Much Freedom for Engineers?" *Machine Design*, Vol. 33 (1961), No. 23, pp. 150–151.

5. G. Gemmill and D. L. Wileman, "The Power Spectrum in Product Management," *Sloan Management Review* (Fall 1970), pp. 15–23.

6. R. R. Ritti, *The Engineer in the Industrial Corporation* (New York: Columbia University Press, 1971), p. 106.

7. Ibid., p. 105.

8. C. Argyris, *Organization and Innovations* (Homewood, Ill.: Irwin-Dorsey, 1965), p. 288.

9. A. W. Blackburn, "Soaring Defense Costs . . . Blame It on the System," *New York Times*, April 1, 1973, sec. 3, p. 3.

10. The interrelationships between communication influence and uncertainty are discussed by Ritti, op. cit. (ref. 6).

11. Margulies and Raia, op. cit. (ref. 1), p. 46.

12. H. J. Andreas, "Cooperation Among Professional Technical and Nonprofessional Organizations in the Electrical Industry," in "Collective Bargaining for Professional and Technical Employees," conference report of the Institute of Labor and Industrial Relations, University of Illinois, May 20–21, 1965, pp. 2–7.

13. Information on reward climate was obtained from the author's own data and the following sources: G. U. Barrett, B. M. Bass, and J. A. Miller, "Combatting Obsolescence Using Perceived Discrepancies in Job Expectations of Research Managers and Scientists," in S. S. Dubin (Ed.), *Professional Obsolescence* (Lexington, Mass.: Lexington Books, 1971), pp. 59–71; J. Hinrichs, "Applying Motivational Concepts to Updating," paper presented at the International Congress of Applied Psychology, Liege, Belgium, July 1971; J. P. Siegel and E. E. Ghiselli, "Managerial Talent, Pay, and Age," *Journal of Vocational Behavior*, Vol. 1 (1971), pp. 129–135.

14. For a discussion of the dual ladder see F. H. Goldner and R. R. Ritti, "Professionalization as Career Immobility," *American Journal of Sociology*, Vol. 72 (1967), pp. 489–502.

15. H. A. Shepard, "The Dual Hierarchy in Research," *Research Management*, Vol. 1 (1958), p. 184.

16. Goldner and Ritti, op. cit. (ref. 14), p. 495.

17. For a discussion of organizational change and development see F. P. Doyle, "Job Enrichment Plus OD—A Two-Pronged Approach at Western Union," in J. R. Maher, *New Perspectives in Job Enrichment* (New York: Van Nostrand Reinhold, 1971), pp. 193–209; Ritti, op. cit (ref. 6).

18. R. L. Kahn, D. M. Wolfe, R. P. Quinn, J. D. Snock, and R. A. Rosenthal, *Organizational Stress* (New York: Wiley, 1964), p. 289.

19. Goldner and Ritti, op. cit. (ref. 14), p. 496.

20. E. E. Ghiselli and D. A. Johnson, "Need Satisfaction, Man-

agerial Success and Organizational Structure," *Personnel Psychology*, Vol. 23 (1970), pp. 577–590.

21. For discussions of functional, product, and matrix forms of organizations see J. R. Galbraith, "Matrix Organizational Designs: How to Combine Functional and Project Forms," *Business Horizons*, Vol. 14 (February 1971), pp. 29–40; A. H. Walker and J. W. Lorsch, "Organizational Choice: Product vs. Function," *Harvard Business Review*, Vol. 46 (November-December 1968), pp. 129–138.

Chapter 7

1. S. J. Oleon, "Changing Patterns in Continuing Education for Business," Center for the Study of Liberal Education for Adults, Boston University, 1967, p. 6.

2. Ibid., chap. 1.

3. The information in this section is based on unpublished data in the possession of the author and the following sources: S. S. Dubin, E. Alderman, and H. L. Marlow, *Managerial and Supervisory Educational Needs of Business and Industry in Pennsylvania* (University Park, Pa.: Department of Planning Studies, Continuing Education, Pennsylvania State University, 1967); F. Landis, "Continuing Engineering Education—Who Really Needs It?" Report C-69-2, November 1, 1969, NYU grant NGR-33-016-017, NASA; W. K. LeBold, R. Perrucci, and W. Howland, "The Engineer in Industry and Government," *Journal of Engineering Education*, Vol. 56 (1966), pp. 237–259; R. Perrucci and J. E. Gerstl, *Professional Without Community: Engineers in American Society* (New York: Random House, 1969); R. Renck, *Continuing Education for R&D Careers*, NSF 69-20, National Science Foundation, June 1969.

4. Renck, op. cit., p. 140.

5. The information on graduate courses and obsolescence was obtained from S. Cenko, "Factors in Obsolescence of Engineering Knowledge," master's thesis, Sloan School of Management, MIT, 1964; G. W. Dalton and P. H. Thompson, "Accelerating Obsolescence of Older Engineers," *Harvard Business Review*, Vol. 40 (September-October 1971), pp. 57–67; H. G. Kaufman, "Work Environment, Personal Characteristics and Obsolescence of Engineers," grant 91-34-69-23, Department of Labor, Office of Manpower Management, June 1970, Clearing-

house for Federal Scientific and Technical Information Report PB 192273; LeBold et al., op. cit. (ref. 3); R. Perrucci and R. Rothman, "Obsolescence of Knowledge and the Professional Career," in R. Perrucci and J. E. Gerstl (Eds.), *The Engineers and the Social System* (New York: Wiley, 1969), pp. 247–275; I. M. Rubin and H. G. Morgan, "A Projective Study of Attitudes Toward Continuing Education," *Journal of Applied Psychology*, Vol. 51 (1967), pp. 453–460.

6. B. G. Davis and E. C. Koerper, "Catch On and Catch Up," *Mechanical Engineering*, Vol. 87 (1965), No. 8, p. 14.

7. J. D. Mooney, "An Analysis of Unemployment Among Professional Engineers and Scientists," *Industrial and Labor Relations Review*, Vol. 19 (1966), p. 525.

8. R. P. Loomba, "A Study of the Re-employment and Employment Experiences of Scientists and Engineers Laid Off from 62 Aerospace and Electronics Firms in the San Francisco Bay Area During 1963–1965," Manpower Research Group, Center for Interdisciplinary Studies, San Jose State College, February 15, 1967, pp. 52, 53.

9. Perrucci and Rothman, op. cit. (ref. 5), p. 273.

10. Renck, op. cit. (ref. 3), p. 66.

11. Ibid., p. 68.

12. See Kaufman, op. cit. (ref. 5); Oleon, op. cit. (ref. 1); Renck, op. cit. (ref. 3).

13. Dalton and Thompson, op. cit. (ref. 5), p. 64.

14. Renck, op. cit. (ref. 3), p. 41.

15. Ibid., p. 72.

16. Ibid.

17. Ibid., p. 76.

18. E. A. Wheeler, "Education for Anti-obsolescence?" *Training and Development Journal*, Vol. 22 (1966), No. 6, pp. 21–26.

19. C. Argyris, *Organization and Innovation* (Homewood, Ill.: Irwin-Dorsey, 1965), p. 228.

20. R. Ritti, *The Engineer in the Industrial Corporation* (New York: Columbia University Press, 1971), p. 216.

21. Kaufman, op. cit. (ref. 5).

22. N. Margulies and A. Raia, "Scientists, Engineers and Technological Obsolescence," *California Management Review*, Vol. 10 (1967), No. 2, pp. 43–48.

23. Renck, op. cit. (ref. 3), p. 137.

24. The survey approach to assessing continuing education needs has been designed and utilized by Donald D. French of Northeastern University, and its development is continuing in collaboration with the author.

25. E. J. Tangerman, "You Say I'm Technically Obsolescent: How Do I Update?" *Product Engineering*, Vol. 35 (1964), No. 18, p. 76.

26. E. F. Obert, "The Little Red School House," Department of Mechanical Engineering, University of Wisconsin, Madison, Wis., undated, p. 1.

27. For a more extensive discussion of self-learning see W. R. Dill, W. B. S. Crowston, and E. J. Elton, "Strategies for Self-Education," *Harvard Business Review*, Vol. 43 (November-December 1965), pp. 119–130.

28. G. S. Odiorne, *Personnel Administration by Objectives* (Homewood, Ill.: Irwin, 1971), chap. 15; D. A. Tagliere, "Training by Objectives," *Manage*, Vol. 23 (September 1970), No. 10, pp. 6–11.

29. For some of the latest trends in educational technology see J. M. Biedenbach and L. P. Grayson (Eds.), *Proceedings Third Annual Frontiers in Education Conference* (New York: IEEE, 1973). For discussion of the positive effects of combining lectures with self-study see J. T. Fitch, "Continuing Engineering Education Through Self-Study," Center for Advanced Engineering Study, MIT, 1971; H. G. Kaufman, "A Review of Research in Independent Study and Implications for Continuing Professional Education," *Journal of Continuing Education and Training*, Vol. 2 (August 1972), No. 1, pp. 1–7.

30. For the effects of time provided for self-development on organizational commitment see Dalton and Thompson, op. cit. (ref. 5), and Renck, op. cit. (ref. 3).

31. Dalton and Thompson, op. cit. (ref. 5), p. 64.

32. For further information on information management see A. W. Wells (Ed.), *Technical Information Center Administration* (Washington, D.C.: Spartan, 1964).

33. P. F. Drucker, "New Technology," *New York Times*, April 8, 1973, sec. 3, p. 6.

34. For discussion about lack of assessment see Renck, op. cit. (ref. 3), and Wheeler, op. cit. (ref. 18).

35. Wheeler, op. cit. (ref. 18), pp. 25–26.

36. M. J. Gannon and J. P. Noon, "Management's Critical Deficiency," *Business Horizons*, Vol. 14 (February 1971), p. 49.
37. D. L. Billiet et al., "Top Management Looks at Loss of Motivation, Overpromotion, Manager Obsolescence," Graduate School of Business, Stanford University, August 1961, p. 55.

Chapter 8

1. S. S. Dubin and D. M. Cohen, "Motivation to Update from a Systems Approach," *Engineering Education*, Vol. 60 (January 1970), No. 5, p. 366.
2. J. G. Roney, *Report on First Conference on Occupational Obsolescence* (Menlo Park, Calif.: Stanford Research Institute, August 1966), p. 11.
3. Ibid., pp. 11–12.
4. "Eleven Doctors Ousted by Medical Group," *New York Times*, January 9, 1972, p. 63.
5. R. Perloff, "Educational Inhibitors and Facilitators of Professional Updating," paper presented at the XVII International Congress of Applied Psychology, Liege, Belgium, July 1971.

INDEX

ability, *see* knowledge acquisition

age, 29, 45–51, 83–87, 140–143
  ability and, 52–53
  initiative and, 100
  motivation and, 53–54, 84
  professional competence and, 46–47
  reward systems and, 124
  risk-taking and, 65–67

Assessment Center Program for Evaluating Supervisory Potential, 77

assessment centers, 76–78, 161

attitude surveys, 33–34, 156

Bell System, 90–92

business professionals, 8–9, 26–27

career change, 57–61, 101–102, 161

career counseling and assessment, 81–83, 101, 149–150, 161

career-goal differences, 57–61

career goals, changes in, 57–61

career path, 82

challenge in work, 90–100, 106

change, 1–3
  in energy and initiative of professionals, 61–62
  in job assignments, 98–111
  occupational, 2
  organizational, 2, 126–128, 131–132
  response to, 64–67
  technological, 1

communication and interaction, 113–115, 121–123

computer professionals, 9–10, 26–27

computers, 1
  continuing-education needs and, 148–149
  information retrieval and, 155

continuing education, 133–159
  effectiveness of, 155–157
  federal government and, 167–168
  integration of goals with, 146–155
  objectives of (table), 134
  planning methods of, 146–157
  professional societies and associations and, 165–167

critical incident technique, 34

3